The Alien Book of Truth

Who Am I?
What Am I Doing?
Why Am I Here?

By Ida M. Kannenberg

Wild Flower Press
Tigard, Oregon U.S.A.
1993

COVER DESIGN: David K. Brunn

David Brunn received his M.F.A. from the University of Oregon in 1986. He began designing art on the Macintosh when the machine was first released in 1984. The process Dave uses to create his artwork is a technique called "stitching" his own photographs together using Adobe's Photoshop on the Macintosh. His inspiration for the designs, of course, comes from within.

COLOPHON

This book was created using Apple Macintosh® IIci, IIcx computers, Quark Xpress® 3.1 software, and an Apple LaserWriter® II NTX. The body style is New Century Schoolbook 10 point on 13-point leading. The cover design was produced with Aldus FreeHand®.

Library of Congress Cataloging-in-Publication Data
Kannenberg, Ida M., 1914-
    The alien book of truth: Who am I? What am I doing? Why am I here? /
    by Ida M. Kannenberg
        p.   cm.
        ISBN 0-926524-15-1: $7.95
    I. Identity.
    II. Individuality
    III. Title.
BC199.I4K36   1993
131----dc20   93-18117
                               CIP

Library of Congress Catalog Card Number 91-6750
First Edition: 1993

The Alien Book of Truth
Copyright © 1993 by Ida M. Kannenberg. All rights reserved.

                    Address all inquiries to :   **Wild Flower Press**,
                                          P. O. Box 230893,
                                          Tigard, Oregon, U.S.A. 97281.

                                  Printed in the U.S.A.
                 This book has been printed on recycled paper.

This book is dedicated to
my patient and enduring
daughter:
Lee Kirk

And to my patient and
endeared husband:
William Kannenberg

Photo by Douglas Newman

Ida Kannenberg:
❖ Came from a book-loving family and, like all budding writers, often spent what should have been food money for books.

❖ Has spent a lifetime puzzling over strange and inexplicable circumstances that life seems determined to impose.

❖ Has left a trail of overflow books behind after 77 years of moving about the western United States.

❖ Is now a proud great-grandmother living by a woods in the outskirts of a small city. She continues to accumulate more books than the apartment will hold.

❖ Continues to search always for reasons and purposes behind the strange and unexplained.

Table of Contents

	Introduction	1
Chapter 1	Existence & Identity	7
Chapter 2	And the Word was God	13
Chapter 3	The Primal Force	21
Chapter 4	Phases of Extension	31
Chapter 5	Fields	35
Chapter 6	True Space and True Time	43
Chapter 7	Waves	51
Chapter 8	Identity	59
Chapter 9	Extension in Space and Time	63
Chapter 10	Finding Ourselves	73
Chapter 11	Development of Individual Identity	81
Chapter 12	Vital Desires	89
Chapter 13	Evaluation and Moral Freedom	101
Chapter 14	The In-forming Spirit	111
Chapter 15	Conclusion	115
Chapter 16	Afterword	121
	Special Acknowledgments	125
	God Dreams, a poem	127
	Affirmation	128

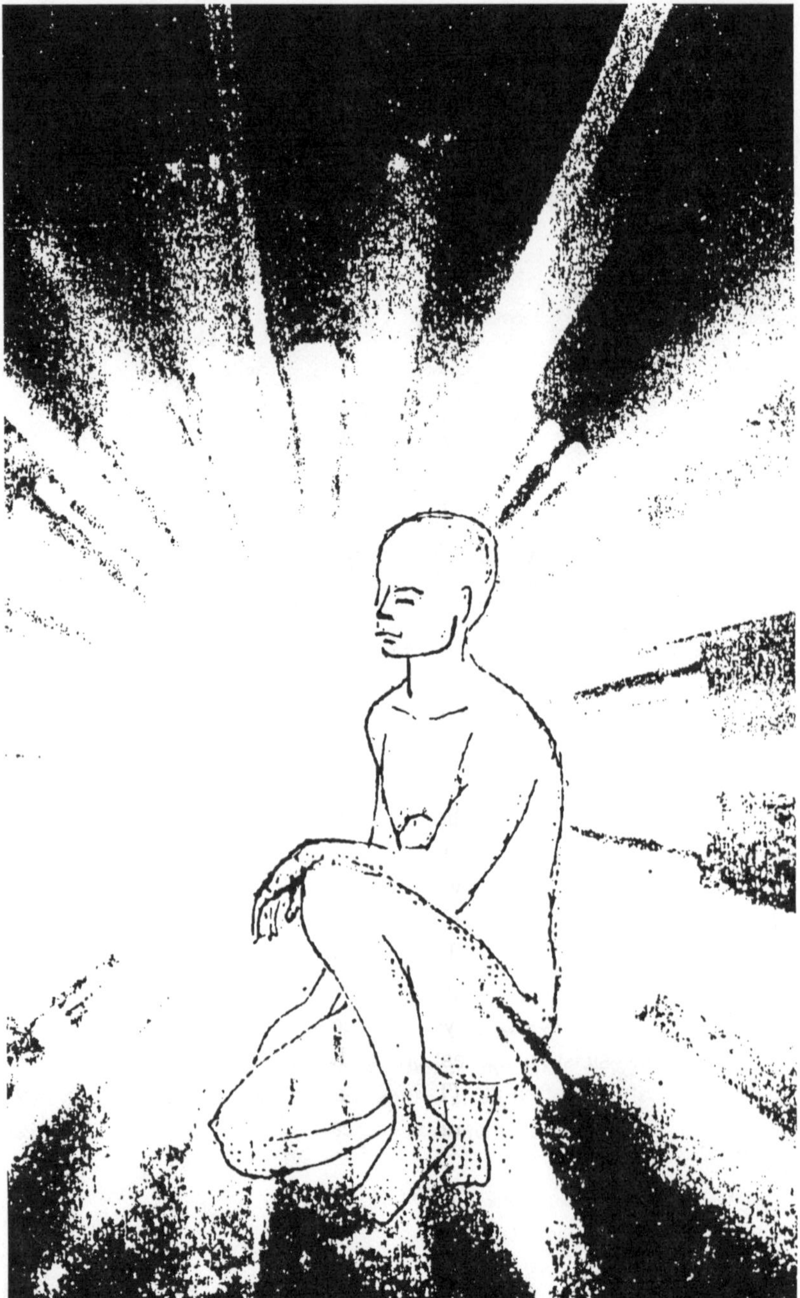

Introduction

Why, who makes much of miracles? As to me I know of nothing but miracles!
　　　　　　　Walt Whitman—*Miracles*

This writing is the result of a study that began about 1930 when I was 15 and still in high school. There were so many questions that needed answers, "Is there God? Who am I? What am I doing? Why am I here?"

I read everything I could get my hands on—religion, philosophy, ancient history, science, anthropology, psychology and all the rest. My notebooks grew fat.

As I read the conflicting and confusing books, sometimes an answer to a question would insinuate itself full blown into my mind. It would have nothing to do with what I was reading. I could "feel" the truth in it and would hasten to write it down before it could evaporate.

Sometimes I would awaken in the night with an answer in my head. I learned to keep pen, paper and flashlight under my pillow.

Today it is over 60 years since that long ago beginning. Today quantum physicists are questioning the idea that every effect proceeds from an antecedent cause. (Their quantum leap has them hanging on a hook). Albert Einstein stuck with cause and effect. I do too. It is by no means a "dead theory."

In 1968 I was the terrified recipient of interior voices. When my terror was realized, this contact was withdrawn.

In 1977 the interior voices returned in a nonterrifying manner, and their unseen owners established a friendly and productive relationship.

One day, June 8, 1978, I mentioned my previous writings to these new friends, and at their request I read them some from my notebooks. They responded by dictating the following, and I wrote it down verbatim:

"We hardly know how to comment on what you have just read to us. It is staggering in its implications. Even our knowledge of this subject is too limited.

"Where have you been hiding your notebook so long? These thoughts are too valuable to hide in a trunk. A great deal of truth and a great understanding is revealed. Some ideas are a little tangled and need to be worked on, but there is so much of value here, it must be brought to light. Yes, later, but the time is approaching fast when it can be appreciated.

"Why don't you open your notebook to your outline? There was something I wanted to re-read. It is the part about spontaneity near the beginning.

"Ida! What have we here? Read that again, more slowly. Great God! That is us!

"Why must we explain ourselves to you? You already know us as well as we know ourselves. Slow down.

"I am the Nameless One, the one you call the Hidden One, yet I do not know more than this outline discloses about the basic nature of reality. Where did you get this material?

"You are only our own dear Ida, but this writing is incredible for someone from your area of being. We know these principles and exist by them, but they should be hidden from your vision. You are right, you have been 'seeing' into our area. We have not been able to explain that entirely to our satisfaction. Now this. Let us read a little more.

"This is too much to take in so fast. I am speechless. It is as though you had written *our Book of Truth!*"

I was wondering what all this was about. Malarkey? Trying to softsoap me into thinking I am more than I am? But something even more strange was about to occur, for then a new dictation was given:

"Be at peace. No harm shall come to you. You have written well what has been given you. Soon the time will come to share it with the world, yea with two worlds, your own and the companion one you have discovered."

Then the previous ones commented:

"You have been visited by a very powerful force. He helped you with the outline and will help you further. We too will help. No, he is not from our world, nor from yours. He is from worlds beyond worlds."

Subsequently my unseen friends urged me to undergo hypnotic regression so that I might discover previous contacts.

In 1980 this was done with Dr. R. Leo Sprinkle of Laramie, Wyoming. It was revealed that in 1940 I had been taken aboard an alien craft, presumably extraterrestrial. This episode and its many years of consequences can be thoroughly explored in another book (See UFOs and the Psychic Factor, Wild Flower Press, 1992), but a short exposition may be in order here.

Just before midnight on December 22, 1940, three men and I were driving eastward on California highway 10 between Indio and Blythe. When we first saw a deep red glow, we thought it was from a distant forest fire. What at first appeared to be an elliptical, then a round, flaming object rose over the horizon; we decided it must be the full moon rising. Later I learned the full moon had occurred ten days earlier, and indeed later that night we saw a quarter moon, which was proper at that time.

The driver pulled over and stopped, and the three men went down the road ahead. I thought I dozed for the hour they stood talking. But many years later when I went under hypnosis it was revealed that two strange men had come to the car. By a ruse they had enticed me to go with them, saying I was badly needed to help someone who had been injured.

I still cannot "see" even under hypnosis all that happened on board the UFO. At the time I took it to be a round cabin of some sort.

All I can recall clearly is that implants, tiny wafer-like objects, were pressed into each ear, one into the left nostril, and by removing the right eye one was inserted into the frontal lobe. I have been told that these implants were comparatively "primitive" compared to those given other persons later. Once the implants were activated they allowed the people of the UFO to "see through my eyes and hear through my ears." I am not sure when activation first took place, right at the time of insertion or as late as 1968.

My brain implant has purposes I have not been told. I do know that it allows them to control my muscular system. I've had enough evidence of that! I am fearful of its total implications and of how and how much it may interfere with my thought processes. The total effect is to make me feel like a wound-up toy.

I have no clue as to whom should be given credit for having helped me discover answers to my questions over these long, slow years. My UFO friends tell me—with a chuckle—"You have friends in high places." That could mean whatever we choose to make of it. Let us control our imaginations. They have also told me they had "scanned" me long before the 1940 contact; it was no accident.

During the 1980 hypnosis sessions I was also made to recall a face-to-face confrontation with the same two men who had taken me from the car. This very early episode took place in 1922 when I was seven years and seven months old, to be exact. At that time the two men had told me to "learn to write well" and to "study people, why they do what they do and what they mean besides what they say." This had been told to me in some subconscious, unheard fashion.

Another recall under that same session was events of my blue-baby death during birth and a rebirth after my maternal grandmother had given me mouth-to-mouth resuscitation. (The inebriated doctor had already left). A second personality came into the same body. This strange mystery must be explored at another time. For me it solves the "Why me" question, only to replace it with "Well then, Who am I?" Under hypnosis that day I said, "It is not time to know, not until all the others are called upon to know, and they are many!"

It seems that every step I take to clear up one of these mysteries only reveals still deeper mysteries. For the time being I must leave them as they are.

These aliens claim that my writing, herein presented, contains their "Book of Truth," but they also deny that they had any part in helping me to write it.

Only the mysterious voice that interrupted our conversation with his own dictation claims to have helped.

He still speaks to me occasionally when I am in some troublesome quandary, always prefacing his remarks with "Be at peace. No harm shall come to you." I hear these words in a low and powerful inner voice.

There is no clue as to whom he might be. The aliens do not reveal whatever they might know. I accept him as some kind of guardian or overseer of both the aliens and myself. I have to believe him to be real because the results of his "presence" are real.

Quantitative measurement has become the function of physical science. Religions are expressed in poetic allusions. Analysis or distillation of abstract principles becomes philosophy. Unfortunately these have become three distinct languages, each bristling at the approach of the other. I am trying to braid the three together to reinforce one concept. I have not invented new ideas so much as interlocked old ones in new ways, giving each added dimensions.

For the most part I have used the pronoun "we" as being most conducive to drawing the reader into a collaborative effort of thought. I could have used "you and I" equally well, or "my potential readers and I" or even included some inspirational guides by saying, "My readers and I and all those who inspired my thoughts, known and unknown." The collective "we" is such a time-saving contrivance that I use it without further apology or explanation.

In what follows I will be using the word "man" to mean any human being, not just those of male gender. Also I will refrain from the distraction of using "he/she" when a generic "he" will suffice. I intend no offense to any of my sisters in this world. As you will see, we will be getting into deep waters, and we need to streamline our communications, or we will all sink like rocks.

CHAPTER

1

Existence & Identity

*To me the converging objects of the universe perpetually flow.
All are written to me and I must get what the writing means.*
            Walt Whitman—*Song of Myself*

One must act effectively in order to live effectively, i.e., usefully and without too much suffering. Obviously, one must think effectively in order to act effectively. Let us assume that most persons want to do precisely that–live usefully and without too much suffering.

Still, living effectively is not enough for the "ego" of a man. He also wants to make his personal identity known, to have it recognized by his fellows and to have it "mean something." He wants it to wield enough power that it will be remembered kindly, or at least remembered, by posterity.

Furthermore, a man wants to feel that his "identity" has some reality of being that in some way it is indestructible or immortal. Once he has recognized himself as existing, he cannot bear to think of himself as not existing forever somewhere and somehow.

What then is a man's reality of being or of identity? How does he come to it, and what becomes of it when the physical body dies?

The purpose of this book is to determine what it means to live, to act, to think effectively, to be recognized and to attain reality of self. This study tells only what it means to do it, not explicitly how to do it. That is the individual's problem.

The most revealing way of explaining a thing is to determine its cause. However, for complete understanding, this would in turn call for an analysis of the cause of the cause, until one might go on and on to the primal cause of all being. Meanwhile, the study would give us no more than a series of effects in reverse order and would draw us further and further away from the subject-effect we wished to study.

Would it not be more satisfactory then, to hypothesize a *primal cause*, and to determine if its nature is such that all effects might follow, down to the present subject-effect we wished to understand? There would be no need to trace or demonstrate each step-by-step cause and effect, but only to ascertain the nature of the primal cause, the pattern of development and the principles and powers by which, and through which, development has been possible.

To start then, we must hypothesize some rational, reasonable, possible and apparent nature of the primal cause of all reality. Then we may try to ascertain man's relationship to the pattern of development, and come at last to some answers to our previously proposed questions.

We start by hypothesizing that: "In the beginning nothing existed except a force of composite nature."

We shall call this force the force of extension, or the force of creation, evolution, and spiritual consciousness. It is this force of extension that works to create the universe. From our human viewpoint we could imagine the force as a great cosmic equation, working itself out in creation and inevitability. The force is the power by which it works, the directives according to which it works, and the material upon which it works.

The important and difficult thing we must do here is to abandon our individual human viewpoint and try to think of the force as it exists in itself and from what would be its own viewpoint.

If you ask where the force came from, or why, or how it was able to be when nothing else was, I can only say that it was, by its nature, not uncaused, but self-caused, and it came into fullness of being through a spontaneous self-creation. If you ask how it came by its nature, I do not know. I do know that if we assume its existence, and nothing more, we can trace a pattern of development for all reality from the force down to the words we are now using and the way we are now thinking. That is quite substantial for one hypothesis.

Science has asked how and when and where in the scheme of things life came into "inert matter." Herein we state what is obvious to us: what came first was life, or rather a living force, and that "inert matter" was a later event.

Although a thing exists solely of its own nature and being, the only way in which we may discuss it is through an ordered sequence of facets, or evaluations, which reduces the thing from reality to the terms of our understanding.

In order to grasp the complete reality of the force of extension, a problem arises because we must try to conceive of it from its own viewpoint of self-creation and eternal existence. But we can only describe it from the conventional terms of our viewpoint of things, which is at the opposite end of creation, looking back. Once we view creation from the viewpoint of the force itself, all that had seemed mysterious, illogical, and irrational from our viewpoint becomes completely natural, logical, and rational.

This does not mean that reality exists only in our delineation or imagination. It means that to be recognized or accepted by our understanding, reality must be reduced to terms intelligible to our understanding. In the reduction, the wholeness of the reality inevitably escapes us. We can only hope to capture enough of its facets so that the escaped wholeness may be intuitively acknowledged to some extent.

If we had different kinds of minds, or imaginations, we could imprison reality in other facets of observation and call the whole actuality something entirely different. Since what we are trying to do is to make the process understandable to our imaginations, we must use the conventional symbols and terms which communicate with our imaginations. It would not profit us much to distort our imaginations into a whole new language of symbolism in order to reveal the actuality in what would only be another, but not necessarily a clearer, language.

So we shall use the symbolism and terms we already have, trying to choose the sharpest, clearest, most penetrative, concise and illuminating terms we can find.

Above all, we strive to use the quiet terms, those which may appeal to reason, and we deliberately avoid using the emotionally loaded ones, no matter how exactly a more traditional term might fit our meaning.

Pinning labels on a thing can be quietly disastrous. One might hesitate to call a spade a spade and then alternate between calling it a trowel and a steam shovel. The instant we label something "A" we have lost a good tenth of our listeners who abhor anything labeled "A" and wouldn't listen with a ten-foot ear. If we call the same item "B," we have lost a different one-tenth, for the same kind of reason.

Using our five senses or the super fine instruments that extend those senses, empirical science measures our experiences with quantitative things.

To study qualitative existences, such as identity and evaluation, we resort to dialectic. Without language, we could have no shared knowledge, no social communication, no storing of information and no civilization or culture. Without language and its labels, knowledge is chaos.

Since we must for reference' sake assign some sort of labels, however inadequate to the entire meaning, we shall make labels in the best fashion we can conceive.

We can name this "force" anything we choose, according to the way our minds are receptive to the notion. We can call it the force of this or the force of that. We can call it life, or God, or Living Spirit, or Immutable Law. Each label we give it but outlines the extent of our ignorance. But in order to discuss it at all, we must call it something, as a point of reference and as a touchstone where we may begin our journey of exploration. From this point we may measure distances and gauge directions, thereby seeing relationships of various facets of existence as they come into discussion. For consistency's sake, we shall refer to the force as *the force of extension*, since that is its function.

We must recall again and again, as we progress, that the reality itself is concrete, and our terms describing it are the abstractions. These necessary abstractions do not in any way negate the concreteness of the reality itself.

Our entire recognition of existence can only equal the sum total of our identity and experience. Experience is quantitative; it functions in space. Identity is qualitative; it functions in time.

All we are really conscious of is our own "selves" and our selves' experiences. We can surmise that other beings that are similar to ourselves in some observable ways are similar to us in other ways as well. We can bring anything into some abstract relationship to our understanding. This is imagination; it is not knowledge.

Knowledge is the change that occurs in our being when some experience passes through it so completely as to cause an irreversible change. The experience must be one of actuality and not of imagination. If it is one of imagination, the change can be completely reversed and corrected by other future experiences of a conflicting or opposing nature and significance. The experience and change can be physical, emotional, intellectual, psychic or spiritual.

From our individuated viewpoint, the *self* objectively indicates our quantitative being, physical body or spatial existence. *Identity* indicates the subjective idea we have of ourselves existing, the recognition or consciousness that we do exist and are individuals. This recognition, or intuition of self-being, is what preserves the identity intact and does not permit it to be destroyed or dispersed. Once we recognize, or formulate, our idea of identity, we strive to maintain it. It is not necessarily any particular idea we have about ourselves; it is only the recognition that we each exist as an individual of a certain kind of nature. It is our "time" being, not temporal of this world only, but our being relative to eternity. It is qualitative being.

That which is quantitative is measured and described in spatial terms. That which is qualitative is measured and described in temporal terms. Understanding of self depends on quantitative distinctions; understanding of identity depends on qualitative distinctions. It is the individual self as quantitative being that experiences and absorbs any experience, whether it be physical, emotional, mental or intuitive. It is the identity as qualitative being which evaluates the experience and extends it as conscious knowledge.

It is identity acting through the self that reveals or illuminates the resultant knowledge. This will not be pure knowledge or absolute fact, for it will be shaped, colored and distorted according to the mind's preheld patterns of perception, regardless of how exact or objective that mind tries to be. A work of knowledge will inevitably be shaped and constricted by the mind from which it comes. Therefore, the irreversible change as originally wrought is, in its expression or realization, always subject to correction, rebalancing and extension. But it is not subject to complete reversal, or else the original evaluation was not knowledge but only imagination or opinion.

Mind is the organ of symbolism; it functions as intellect. Identity is the organ of evaluation; it functions as will.

We can think of "mind" only when we think of it in action after the fact of experience, in thinking about or abstracting symbols and ideas from experience. The senses of the physical body and the physical brain are the organs of perception. Identity and mind are nonmaterial, but they are reality nonetheless. They translate and evaluate. The evaluation is relative truth i.e., relative to the power of perception of the self and to the quality of evaluation of the identity.

Science and mathematics merely increase enormously the number of relative truths known. They slice them into finer texture and impose on them some order or pattern agreeable to man's understanding, in comparison to some other thing. But in no way do they demonstrate the nature of the thing studied in its own reality.

No matter how hard or in what manner we search for truth, we can never reach more than a relative truth, for knowledge is interpreted according to our capacity of perception, assimilation, emotional bent of acceptance and tools and symbols of understanding.

There is, however, one path of true knowledge that grasps the true being and essence of a subject all at once, and this we generally call *intuition*. Intuition cannot be forced, and the more accurate it is the less exactly it can be defined into and communicated through words. The knowledge it reveals can be used as a tool to dig for knowledge of a more translatable kind, as an illumination for a new path of inquiry, or most valuably as inspiration and encouragement to the one making the inquiry.

Intuition seems to pertain mostly to the recognition of the nature of the thing or the underlying principles that hold a thing together. It pertains to what makes it what it is, to its personal equation or formula of being, and to its reality. Everyone has and uses intuition to a greater or lesser extent, but as often as not each of us fails to recognize that it is intuition.

Experiences of knowledge, imagination, and intuition were all used and are apparent in the formulation and narration of this study. We are not trying to find some magical proposition by which we can control the universe. We are trying to find some means of understanding our human predicament, and perhaps, through understanding, come to some acquiescence to, or even to some rebellion from, our personal circumstances.

Armageddon is even now being fought daily in the world, not on the battlefields, but in the minds of those who try to determine, on a rational basis, what life, liberty, and death are all about. We seek useful understanding , not a monument.

CHAPTER

2

And the Word was God

These are really the thoughts of all men in all ages and lands, they are not original with me.
          Walt Whitman—*Song of Myself*

The first impetus for this study happened when I was about eight or nine years old. I came home waving a Sunday School paper and asked, "Mama, what was the Word?"

"Word? What word?" She was perplexed.

"You know. Our lesson says, 'In the beginning was the Word, and the Word was with God, and the Word was God.'" *(John* 1:1)

"Oh!" She laughed. "The Word was God. It tells you right here." She pointed. "The Word was God."

I thought about that, but I wasn't satisfied.

"Then why doesn't it just say, 'God was'?" I was never one to waste words; the fewer the better was my contention.

My pretty Mama (who never knew she was pretty) smiled indulgently and replied, "I guess just to make little girls ask questions."

I should have known that would be my answer.

Certain that there was some secret or esoteric meaning in the Word, I began a long, long train of thought. I detested secrets. Secrets were an insult. Knowledge was meant to be shared.

I can't say the question was on my mind constantly or that I lay awake thinking about it, but now and then I again asked myself, "What was the Word?" There was another meaning there besides just God, there was a duality, the Word *and* God.

By the time I reached high school I was introduced to the philosophers, the easier ones, and I began to write out my ideas and questions. I decided Word meant idea. "In the beginning was the idea, and the idea was with God, and the idea was God."

Hmph. It was not exactly an elegant improvement, but it offered more significance as a springboard to thought.

Eventually I discovered that the original St. John's testament was written in Greek, and in Greek word was logos and logos meant concept or thought, and *also the utterance or expression of that concept or thought.*

So what was the concept? There was God the Self, and God's concept of Self and the expressions of that concept of Self. I didn't know it, but I had just encapsulated all the heavens and universes in a nutshell!

The words of Baruch Spinoza (Dutch, 1632-1677) stuck with me: "God knows," said Spinoza. "And what He knows is Himself."

I saw the Self (God) and the concept of Self (the Word) as a duality, and there was also the triad of the original statements:
- In the beginning was the Word
- and the Word was with God
- and the Word was God

Why was this said in three different ways? Why in the Old Testament were there three different words for God: Jehovah, Elohim and Adonai? Were these three different expressions of His concept of Self?

I reasoned that the duality and the triad meant that from His viewpoint there were three objective aspects of Self (God) and three subjective aspects of the expression of God's concept of Self (the Word).

I had long before decided that Creation and its laws necessitated the concept of a spiritual force extending into the material world of space and time. I found encouragement in the works of Gottfried Leibnitz (German 1646-1716) philosopher and mathematician.

"There is an analogy, a strict relation, between God's ideas and man's, and identity between God's logic and man's.

> *"If visible movement depends on an imaginary element found in the* concept of extension, *it can no longer be defined by a simple local movement, it must be the result of a force.*
>
> *"...Movement depends on the action of a spirit."*

While I did not adopt Leibnitz' or anyone else's ideas completely, the thoughts of many people gave me clues to the answers I was seeking, and I adapted them to my needs.

I won't put you through all the paces it took for me to resolve to my own satisfaction the questions that the six objective and subjective aspects created for me. Considered from God's own objective viewpoint, His three God aspects would be considered those of His Power, His Being and His Acting. His three Word aspects would be His Identity (recognition of self existence), all extended existences as recognition of Himself, and extended actions of a particular kind.

Pertinent to all this was a verse from *Exodus* 3:14:

"And God said unto Moses, 'I Am that I Am,' and He said, 'Thus shalt thou say unto the children of Israel, 'I Am hath sent me to you.'"

Here He has given Himself personal identification.

"I Am" puts the emphasis on the idea of someone who exists rather than on the idea of that which is existing. It denotes only the original objective Self, it does not release the necessary concepts of extended existences.

"I Am that I Am" adds recognition of self-extension.

We must also note that the "Am" of "I Am" is an active verb from "to be," for it is in the acting that the reality becomes apparent to us as living spirit or force. It thus becomes the third member of the triad, recognized as the third persona of the Trinity.

The Bible and philosophy had brought me this far, but it was not far enough. All I had was words on paper and the recognition that things were getting geometrically complicated. I had a duality, a triad, six aspects and a headache trying to reconcile all the relationships and the acting power (extension) of it all.

One thing that still bothered me in the "I Am that I Am" was the word "that." It was a long time before I found an explanation. Madame Helena Blavatsky (Russia, 1838-1891) wrote in her book *The Secret Doctrine*: "...in the earliest MS of Indian literature this unrevealed abstract Deity has no name. It is generally called 'that.' (Tad in Sanskrit). It means all that is, was, or will be or that can be so received by the human mind." I am sure the "that" in the Biblical quotation was intended to reveal this attribute of allness, infinite and eternal.

I Am—all, infinite, eternal—I Am extended in concepts of being.

Finding labels for the six aspects was the most difficult part of the whole process. One day one category seemed to fit, another day another category seemed right. Finally, trying to bring all possibilities under one cover, I chose the broadest terms possible, intending to extrapolate later the various categories that seemed to whirl in cycles from them.

I had now come to the fringes of science. Acting power—extension—meant a force, and in this case it would be a force of a dual nature, a force of Word and God. Questions by the hundreds hurled themselves at me.

Sometimes the notebooks were buried for many years at a time as marriage, housework and child rearing demanded much attention. Once, in my frustration, I completely destroyed all the notebooks, and several times I partly destroyed them. But there was always a compulsion that brought me back to the study each time, starting over or trying to pick up where I had left off.

One of the philosophers who had enormous impact on my studies was Henri Bergson (French 1859-1941). His ideas of creative evolution, the élan vital (vital impulse) and the "importance of becoming" fit into my understandings of how things are.

"The evolutionary process is the endurance of a vital impulse continually developing and generating new forms in geometric progression" said Bergson, and I found much there to think about. This was very good for evolution. But what if the force that guided *creation* could be captured and defined by the same law? Such a force would exist in isolation, outside space, time and materiality.

Bergson also suggested that we think of the geometry of evolution as an artillery shell bursting, with additional bursts from each original branch. He saw evolution as creative, not mechanistic.

These ideas helped formulate some of the basic tenets of my primal force concept, but it took much prolonged study and many abortive attempts at logic to come to some conclusions about the many questions that arose from it.

To begin with, how was I thinking about force? Could I make any definition of it that would outlast my study?

I decided, "A force is an active stress that plays its impulsions on an object so as to compel it to action of a specific kind, direction or extent."

This definition did not reveal the dynamics of the force I was trying to define, a force which I had come to call "the force of extension."

The break came when I recalled something I had read about Isaac Newton (English, 1643-1727) and his third law of motion

"When two particles interact, the force of each are of equal magnitude but opposite directions, so that forces always appear in equal and opposite pairs."

Since the force of extension exists in isolation outside of space, time and materiality, there cannot be another particle or force of opposite direction unless both of these exist in one dual or composite force that contains within itself the two opposing and equal directives. Since we do not yet have any particles to consider, we conceive of the force carriers as "directives."

Of course it is generally believed that Einstein ruffled the edges of classical physics, especially Newton's laws of motion. But as Sir James Jeans (English, 1877-1946) pointed out, "The theory of relativity deals with the measuring of things, not with their nature." Since we deal with the nature of things, we can safely apply Newton's principle which ultimately exhibits the nature of forces.

Life went on. Much time passed. Studies thickened. Reams of paper were covered with trial and error answers that proved no answers. If an answer led to a deadend instead of an extension of thought, it was thrown out. I knew that there was a natural process of understanding to be found and followed that would reveal many of nature's mysteries.

Dictionaries and the thesaurus were always open, and the finest distinctions were tried. Several of my final choices were lately abandoned as being too esoteric and generally unknown. More common words were substituted, but not without a pang of regret. I tried to be guided by the current mode of speech and understanding, rather than by linguistic text books that sometimes took me somewhat off the track of my intent.

The next big question was how to describe this dual force. By this time I was aware that all creation depended on that duality.

First, in what way was it dual? Were there two concepts skipping happily along side by side agreeing totally with each other? No, no matter how I tried to imagine such coziness, the two always coalesced into one if I thought about them long enough. They had to be in some way and to some extent opposing, but in a controlled and harmonious way. It took a good long while through many false avenues and side trips, but I finally found myself contemplating the yin and yang of Asiatic beliefs. I found it an acceptable exposition of the duality of positive and negative natures.

The Encyclopedia Britannica (Vol. 12 p. 845, latest edition) states:

> "Yin Yang: In Eastern thought the two complementary forces, or principles, that make up all aspects and phenomena of life.
>
> "Yin is conceived of as earth, female, dark, passive, absorbing.
>
> "Yang is conceived of as heaven, male, light, active and penetrating.
>
> "The two are said to proceed from the supreme Ultimate (T'ai Chi); the interplay on one another...being a description of the actual process of the universe and all that is in it. In harmony the two are depicted as the light and dark halves of a circle."

While I had already come to the concept of a force with dual principles, or directives as I called them, I was enormously encouraged by finding this exposition and by the fact that Christian doctrine (John 1:1) and terms of the Hebrew testament (Exodus 3:14) could be conjoined to the Asiatic concept of the Ultimate (yin and yang).

In my pursuit through many religions and doctrines, I had found coherences and consistencies that were surprising. Many of those were displaying the same ideas but with different emphasis and different descriptive words. I grieved that so many have died because of those superficial differences, and the grief energized and emboldened my efforts.

The yin and yang solidified for me the idea of two opposing but interpenetrative directives of one force, and from there it was simply a matter of deciding how these factors would work in harmony to extend all things of nature. All of the above contribute to the definition of what I have called the force of extension.

In my own naive innocence I did not realize that what I was constructing could be called a methodology until I read Georg W. F. Hegel (German, 1770-1831). In his *General Concept of Logic* he revealed "...a dialectical scheme that emphasizes progress of history and ideas from thesis to antithesis and thence to a higher synthesis." He says, "...negation is just as much affirmation as negation...it results in a new concept, a higher richer concept than that which preceded it...On these lines the system of concepts has broadly to be constructed and to go on to completion in a resistless course." Hegel called this his natural method of logic.

In trying to be as logical as I could conceive I had just naturally fallen into something similar to his methodology though instead of talking about thesis and antithesis I was talking about dual and opposing directives in a single force. We agreed however, that all concepts should fit into a natural whole.

So far so good. But how do the sciences of the four dimensional physical universe fit into this methodology? While I came across many analogies between the spiritual and the physical, the border between the two seemed closed, until I began to pick up on quantum physics and the wonderfully strange and active world of particles, photons, quanta, quarks, electrons and leptons. By any other name these would be as sweet, for they brought me over the border. But we must approach all this from the far side.

CHAPTER 3

The Primal Force

Failing to fetch me at first, keep encouraged.
Missing me one place search another
I stop somewhere waiting for you.
            Walt Whitman—*Song of Myself*

A force is an active stress that plays its impulsions on an object, thus compelling it to an action of a specific kind, direction and extent. The force of extension contains within its own power and being seemingly opposing and conflicting necessities of its own existence. Without one or the other of these opposing directives it would be something other than a force. Separated, each of the interpenetrative and coexistent directives would be a principle only. Without the tension of equilibrium of the directives in opposition, there would be no identity, power or being as a force, no sensitivity, no consciousness and no receptivity.

A thing has reality of being if it exists because of its own inherent nature and does not exist solely because of the action of, or relationship to, other things. If it did, it would be "real" as a house or bridge is real due to the relationships of wood and steel and cement, but it would be a relative existence and would be real only from our point of reference in time and space, and would not have reality of being in itself.

The force has reality of being because it exists by the qualities of its own nature, by its own specific directives of function.

The force of extension is that force which impels any existence that has reality of being to
- extend its self (in experience) in such a way that
- its own identity is retained, and yet at the same time
- there must be objectified or manifested a new kind of action, a new force or a new individuation (a new "thing"), which in turn comes into its own identity and its own reality of being. It exists in its own equation of being, or formula of nature, and may thereafter be acted upon by the force.

From our viewpoint in space and time, the force of extension could be called, among other things, the life force, but from its own viewpoint it is living force. It is far more than just a life force. It is all: all being, all power and all consciousness.

Any force exists only when it is in action. There is no such thing as a nonacting or abstract force. Such an abstraction or nonacting force can exist only as a concept in our imaginations, as we catch it for a moment in order to talk about it. The force of extension came into existence with its own first act of self-creation, of self-becoming, a spontaneous, all-at-once action without actual motion.

The force impels action of a definite direction and final purpose in an object, and it is therefore directive, but it does not impel a specific mode of attainment of that final purpose. The attainment is in the action of extension, and that specific mode of attainment is left up to the free will of the individuation or object upon which the force plays its impulsions. The idea of determinism is thus precluded.

The final purpose is specifically determined by the choice made by the free will or nature of the individuation that feels the impulsions of the force.

The final purpose of the force of extension is the same as the primal purpose—extension. The idea of chance is thus precluded.

Because the force forever endures in its own identity even after extension into new individuations, and because the force extends self as impulsions, there is not one simple act of impulsion from the past from which creation mechanically works out. Rather, there is a constantly reissued, rereceived, renewed impulsion, with individual beings drawing at every moment from the living force. The idea of mechanism is thus precluded.

To think of the force of extension in its first spontaneous action of self-becoming or self-creation, we must think of it serving itself in the following self-relations:

- author of action
- directives of action
- energy of action
- object of action
- the impulsions (or whatever kind of energy vibrations, radiation or urges the force acts through)
- the action of transmission of impulsions
- the action of reception of impulsions
- the abstract place in which this occurred (in lieu of space)
- the spontaneity in which this occurred (in lieu of time)
- the wholeness of all this, the absolute reality, the undivided oneness, interpenetration, the allness of the self-contained action without motion *(the Supra-nature)*.

We cannot know this absolute reality of being as it exists in itself, but we can know it as it exists as primal cause of all extended creation.

Simultaneous with this act of self-creation was the initial concept of being, which established identity.

Only the force of extension can be called absolute, and its absoluteness is that of absolute reality. In its own nature it is infinite and eternal. It is without measure, an unlimited potential of becoming or extension. It is infinite in the sense that its sphere of influence is infinite, extending infinitely into all without restraint. It is limited only by the receptivities of that which it acts upon, and it is eternal in that it acts upon every reality that ever was, is, or will be. Even before creation it was itself. We must recognize that such terms as infinite and eternal are literary terms of understanding rather than actual things. That is, there is no such thing as infinity or eternity existing as things in themselves, but there is an infinite and eternal force. There is no such thing as infinite space or eternal time. Such terms are as self-contradictory as a "shoreless lake."

Had the force not created itself in its self-becoming, it would not be infinite and eternal. If something existed prior to and outside of the force that could call it into being and create it, the force would be limited by the exact dimensions of that which called it into being. To be infinite means to be without measure; to measure is to recognize and compare finite quantities. To be eternal is to be without change.

Pre-space is usable as a term to denote that which has no measurable area of being, not because it is infinite, but because it is pre-existent to quantitative being or the possibility of measurement of any kind. Pre-space is the sphere of influence of the force in its primal phase of self-becoming. Pre-space and pre-time are elastic media in that they are coextensive to the actual extension of the force in its processes of self-becoming. They are in some way correspondent to what would be the "field of consciousness" (intellect) of the force from its own viewpoint of becoming, the area in which the "power" functions. With every exercise of consciousness, the field of consciousness expands.

Substance indicates any existence that may be observed in some manner by us or grasped concretely in our imagination in its natural properties or character.

Time is a conventional symbol indicating the measurements of the relationships of various facets of a subject under consideration. It denotes duration and sequence of the facets as we observe or imagine them. Pre-space is not infinite in that it is not yet complete, but neither is it finite, since it is not contained. It is *potential*. Our conventions of time are not reality, but they are real in our imagination as we divide up existence according to our specific purposes. We invent these conventions of time as we need them, to express relationships of limited or quantitatively observable individuations.

There is, however, an actual element of time existing as a reality. Later we shall discuss this more fully. Pre-time, from our viewpoint, exists concurrently with the eternal force, but it marks out the act of self-becoming only, i.e., creation from the viewpoint of the acting force. We must constantly distinguish between the viewpoint of the acting force and our own individuated viewpoint, as they are opposites. What is objective to the force is subjective to us and vice versa.

The directives of the force of extension are coexistent and interpenetrative. Their opposing tendencies, to extend self and to retain identity, are of exactly equal strength and value, which holds them in dynamic equilibrium. The tension of this equilibrium makes them sensitive, that is, capable of being responsive to stimuli. Thus, as coexistent and interpenetrative existence, they may be considered as "that which may be acted upon"—sensitive existence, or some kind of *pre-substance*. This dynamic equilibrium is itself consciousness (sensitivity and self-experience). These directives of the force are also its power of acting. Held in equilibrium, they are its equalized powers, without motion, but with potential of action. We will use *power:being* to represent powerful existence and sensitive existence, that is, will and consciousness.

The composite value of powerful existence and sensitive existence as coexistent and interpenetrative indicates:
- the potential of impulsions by means of which the force impels any reality to extend itself, and
- the potential of some kind of pre-substance as that which is receptive to the impulsions of the force.

The force can extend itself and at the same time retain its full nature identity as power:being only by extending self as impulsions. It extends self through its own power (will) in action according to its own directives. It extends self upon itself as being (consciousness), through processes of *conceptual dissociation*. Simultaneous to the primal act of self-extension as impulsions is the first phase of extension, an act of dissociation of self into conceptual objective and subjective self-relations, the whole recognizing the parts. This dissociation is into objective power and subjective identity, objective being and subjective existence, objective "acting" (in impulsions) and subjective "action" as directives.

This act of self "knowledge" is of exact equal value and occurrence to the act of self-becoming as impulsions and is a kind of congruent doubling of self upon self, subjective reality on objective reality.

These concepts of self-relations, both objective and subjective, are equally infinite and eternal to the impulsions of the self-becoming, but they are *simultaneously coextensive with each other rather than interpenetrative or coexistent*. From the viewpoint of the force, this and all dissociations are only conceptual, not actual divisions. (See Figure 3-1.)

The force of extension can never withhold itself in the minutest degree from its full and complete action upon that which is receptive or sensitive to it. In order to act and at the same time retain its identity, as impulsions, it must act fully and completely, since any

Objective	Subjective
power (will)	identity (force)
being (consciousness)	existence (pre-substance)
acting (impulsions)	action (directives)

Figure 3-1
Conceptual Self-Relations

```
                UNKNOWABLE "THAT"
                   Self-Becoming
                   Self-Relations
                   Supra-nature

   GOD                                    LOGOS
(interpenetrative)   Duality            (coexistent)



   POWER
   (will)                                IDENTITY
                                          (force)
   BEING                                EXISTENCE
(consciousness)                        (pre-substance)
   ACTING
  (impulsions)                            ACTION
                                        (directives)
                   CONTINUES
```

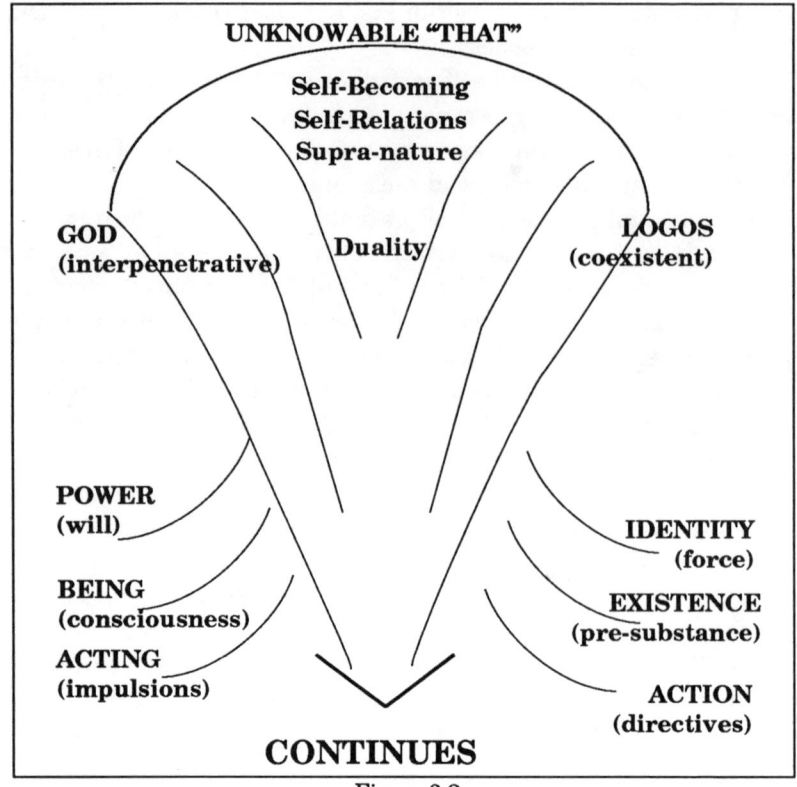

Figure 3-2
Each phase continues to interact with each new extension.

retention of its absoluteness would change its nature identity into some different thing. (See Figure 3-2.)

The force of extension is absolute immutable law, even to itself. We must not argue that seeing the force as immutable law, which even it cannot break in any way, limits or binds restrictions upon it! Because nothing else exists or will ever exist outside of its own existence and nature, there is nothing that can restrict the force. If it ever acted in any way other than by the immutable law of its own nature, it would thereby destroy itself.

Creation was possible at all only because the law and the nature are immutable. The immutability is not restrictive—it is absolute freedom to be, to become, to create and to extend. Imagining a different kind of force, one could imagine a different kind of unisphere (all possible universes), but then you and I would not be here to argue about it. The fact that the law is immutable is evidence of absolute power as well as wisdom.

Whether we relate all these ideas in the quasi-scientific jargon of forces, equations and laws or in the humanistic terms of God and divine attributes depends on our own preferred way of thinking about it, or our own immediate purpose in speaking of it. The truth remains the same, however we describe it. Our words are only symbols of reality.

The conceptual self-relations are something the force knows or recognizes about its own nature. It recognizes them by the process of using them through an act of "will," and in so doing, it gives them their own indestructible identities (concretizes them). The objective power in some way corresponds to what we call "will" in ourselves, and objective being corresponds to what we call "intellect" or consciousness. To the force, each new individuation is simply a new facet of knowledge of itself. Only from our viewpoint is a new individuation discontinuous, and even then it is discontinuous only from other individuations, not from the identity of the force.

A thing acted upon by the force of extension will be able to receive and respond to the full force of extension only according to the degree of its own reality of being, i.e., its own capacity and limitations of reception, evaluation and extension. Once set free or extended as new individuation, that individuation indicates an irreversible change. It cannot be retracted into the prior existence from which it was extended. The prior existence, however, continues in its own being and identity.

It is not a contradiction to say that all extended individuation remains within the actual being of the force and to say that the new individuation cannot be retracted into the prior existence from which it was extended. It is a fact that the new identity as an identity is held and continues forever within the being of the force, which establishes the proof of immortality of identity of extended individuation.

We cannot see or visualize a force—we only see what happens to an object when a force impels it. A thing responds to the force according to the degree in which it partakes of reality, and to the degree to which it is able to accept the impulsions of the force. In so doing, it may appear to be responding to any number of different forces, according to its level or quality of reality. The thing responding thus seems to cut out and utilize from the full extent of the force only as much as it has the capacity to use. This "cutting out" is purely unselfconscious.

As an alternate view, we could say that all the forces of nature are but viewpoints of the full force of extension, limited by the circumstances of individuations through which we observe them acting. Such forces seem to be discontinuous from the action of the full force, not because they are actually separate, but because they are barred from any more complete exhibition of the full force by the individuated form's limitations of acceptance and response.

In "inert" matter, the forces that show through are recognizable as kinds of motion, atomic or molecular. In organic matter the forces "extend" into those of bio-chemistry, of birth, growth and decay. In animal organisms, the new forces becoming apparent are those of sense perceptions. In man the new forces are those of ideas, evaluations, abstractions of experience and free will.

In many instances, the force is not able to extend through the forms of individuations. The forms run into blind alleys of endeavor, block themselves off by using their free will or choice of specific modes of attainment of extension in ways that do not permit further extensions of the force. Millions more are unsuccessful than are successful in serving as further avenues of extensions to the force. They may continue as forms for a long time, but eventually they will be mowed down by circumstances. They cannot evolve.

When the force impels a thing to extend itself, what it is asking, in effect, is that the individuation *collaborate* in what is really further extension of the force's self, since all being has extended from, and remains within, the being of the force. The specific mode of extension is chosen, consciously or instinctively, by the individuated form, and it is accepted or rejected, i.e., evaluated, by the force in that it either does or does not further extend through the chosen extension of the form. The force evaluates automatically but not consciously, because its working is immutable and absolute law, not capricious choosing of yes and no.

Obedience of the individual to the way of extension is rewarded without stint, precisely according to its desserts in absolute justice without error. *This collaboration by the form and evaluation by the force is the significance and the final purpose of the whole process.* It is, in essence, *cocreation*.

The mode through which a form tries to extend itself is possible according to the limitations and capacities of its nature, i.e., its inheritance of being. The ardor with which the form endeavors to extend itself depends on the completeness of reality of its identity, receptivity and response to the force's impulsions and its own (the form's) "estate of consciousness." The success of the extension in the mode chosen further depends on environmental stress and accidents, both beneficial and disastrous, including experience, education of the individuation *and* the form's inheritance of capacities.

CHAPTER

4

Phases of Extension

*I look and behold God in every object
Yet understand God not in the least.*
　　　　　　Walt Whitman—*Song of Myself*

　　　Motion is not a reality of being in itself, but is apparent because of successive changes of position of bodies in space. The bodies change because of the impulsions received from the force of extension.
　　　In phase one, the phase of self-becoming and conceptual self-relationships of the force, we recognized pre-space, the sphere of influence of the force in that phase of being. We also recognized pre-time and pre-substance. There was not yet motion, for there was no actual space to change position in, and no variance of "directions" to make change of position possible. Extension or self-becoming of phase one goes on forever in a "perpetual cycle of equalized change," a motionless action in which the force simultaneously extends self as power (will) and in the same timeless time absolutely and completely receives self in being (consciousness or knowledge).
　　　The transmissions of "self" in this phase of self-becoming were an absolutely complete transmission of self, for that is the only way the nature of the acting force may be retained with its identity intact. It can never withhold itself in the minutest degree from that which is receptive to it. Since it was acting upon itself and is itself absolute reality, it is completely receptive to itself. It must then completely and absolutely receive and absorb self. In this motionless motion and timeless time, the primal act of self-becoming, by its own nature and conditions of being, extends in the congruent doubling of

self. This extension is made possible only by dissociation into the conceptual self-relations of separated objective power:being:acting, and subjective identity:existence:action. Thus, it is instantaneously the same thing for the Supra-nature to conceive or "think" of a thing and to will it into creation. (God said, "Let there be Light," and there was light.)

This experience of simultaneous transmission and reception of self completely in phase one indicates that the Supra-nature has absolute knowledge of all extended individuations. This is not some idea that the Supra-nature has of the extension. It is pure existential knowledge of whatever reality of being the individuation possesses.

All individuated extension is held within the being of the force by the principle of cohesion: the directive of retention of identity. But through the principle of dissociation, individuated extension can be identified in its own individuated being as some new manifested thing. Each new manifested thing appears to the force as a new experience of, or awareness to, itself. The force completely absorbs itself through self-reception in each extension, thus forever balancing the equation. It forever "knows itself" completely.

The manner in which the force expresses its recognition of, or knowledge of, these experiences of self that are "new forms of individuation or creation" is the process of using them for further extension. It is much easier to describe this process as an action (and it is in the action that the reality lies) than it is to give a name to the action, since any term we choose is from our viewpoint of creation. A better term would describe it from the viewpoint of the force itself existing in action.

We might say that it is a kind of evaluation that the force makes of the form (or that which is extended). It evaluates the possibilities of the form for extension by the act of extending itself to the limits of the form, and this action itself is the evaluation, or expression of recognition, of the force for the form.

The action, as self-knowledge, is the force coming into a new recognition or awareness of self in each one of the extended forms of creation.

Before any new individuation throughout creation ever becomes visibly manifest in the material unisphere, it first exists as a conceptual self-relation. Since this phase is outside of space and time, though continuing concurrently to it, we can well believe that each of us, in some way, has first existed as a concept in the pre-time and pre-space phase of being. This concept in some way corresponds to consciousness, but until the process of evaluation, it is a concept of self-relation of the force, not a concept of an individual identity. This dichotomy has tremendous implications for such social issues as abortion and infant baptisms.

In phase two, the only possible mode of extension to that which was already "all existence" was quantitative dissociation of self into conceptual particles of self. In phase two, the extended self is the sensitized pre-substance that extends into particles of sensitized being, or into elemental, indivisible particles

In phase three, the particles could extend themselves only through new kinds of relationships. Self-dissociation of indivisible particles would destroy their identity. Relationships are subatomic and atomic structures.

Phase three, the establishment of new relationships of particles, establishes form within space. Form is the outline of motion within the cohesion of individuated identity.

Phase four of extension carries out the pattern of development possible to that form. It is a qualifying transformation within the form. It is the result of the form extending itself in collaboration with the force's self without destroying the identity of the form. The form's weight of history comes from the repeated impulsions of the force passing through the form, impelling it to extend self in collaboration with the force. The resultant qualifying changes forever give it more tension of being, more sensitivity, more depth of reality, more grace of being and more knowledge. The weight of history is transformative time.

The form's weight of history is the value of all qualifying changes that occur in the history of the form. Not one dot of experience or being ever escapes to be wasted. It is all valued and used in one manner or another. This weight of history is the retention of the force's self, retained through all its qualifying transformations within the form, which is its extension as identity in time, just as form was its extension as being in space.

CHAPTER

5

Fields

Nature is rude and incomprehensible at first. Be not discouraged, keep on, there are divine things well developed. I swear to you there are divine things more beautiful than words can tell.

Walt Whitman—*Song of the Open Road*

A major question had confronted me along the way: how, when and where was the original equilibrium between the directives broken into so that the action of creation could occur? What had I omitted in my calculations? Then came another of those impactive flashes of intuition. It was not the *fact* of equilibrium I should be questioning, it was the *tension* thereof. I had been thinking of equilibrium as aspects of push and pull, positive-negative, and all sorts of opposing contrasts and opposites. But I had not been thinking of the tension except insofar as the tension was what made the force sensitive to stimuli. I had not gone far enough. It was sensitive to stimuli, but the only stimulus around was itself, therefore it had to be self-sensitive or conscious.

While I actually knew better I had been treating the force as inert and static, a statement that I could pin on the wall above my typewriter. I had to recall that its directives were equalized, not inert, and it was potential of enormous power and activity.

I had properly thought of the force as non-material and existing outside of space and time as we generally think of them. The best word to describe that state was "spiritual."

Let us make these definitions:
- Spirit: "the form of being or substance characterized by self-consciousness, self-activity, and personality (specific characteristics) and the absence of distinctly material properties.
- Personality: That which distinguishes or characterizes (a person).
- Identity: (a) (absolute), that which involves exact sameness with itself or self-sameness. (b) the distinctive character belonging to an individual or class.
- To identify: to ascertain the personality, character or relations of.

Therefore "to retain identity" is to recognize and maintain in self-consciousness the particular character or characteristics that makes a specific "it" what "it" is.

The point of release from the tension of equilibrium, as self-consciousness, would be the force recognizing itself as "being" in all its identifying characteristics. This is the time the conceptual self-relations come into focus.

The wholeness of the Supra-nature extends itself as concepts of self, thus dividing the allness into separately distinguishable parts that now may be separately active. Without this conceptual separation further extension or creation would be impossible. This concept is not so difficult to imagine as the words make it seem.

If your child has a string of those plastic pop-apart beads all snapped together in a string, you have a symbol or analogy of the unit of allness. One part cannot act against or independently of another part when all are snapped together. Now take them apart and one section can do all sorts of rude things to any of the other sections. Your child will show you by banging them together or squashing one on top the other until Mother says "Stop that!"

So the conceptual self-relations of the Supra-nature means a separation of parts and actions, and we are well on the way to discovering the physical universe, and maybe a few other universes as well!

Since we don't know exactly how the Supra-nature conceives of its own being, we have to struggle as best we can to make all this recognizable to our imaginations and, we hope, to our understanding. We are suffering the pangs of idea birth; the labor is long and not without pain.

The idea of the whole contemplating its parts introduces the principles of separation and cohesion. The tension of the equilibrium (of the self-creation concept) is unbalanced, and alternation of extension and retention is now conceivable. A kind of turbulence of alternation has been set up.

With further extensions the intervals between the two directives ever widens from interpenetration, to coexistent, to coextensive, to freedom enough to directly oppose each other's commands. This *widening interval principle* is extremely important to the future action and to our understanding.

There is one difference in viewing the Supra-nature contemplating its parts as equivalent to the snap-apart beads. The Supra-nature continues also as a whole even as it considers the parts. The beads of course taken into parts are simply parts, the whole is missing.

Each new phase in the becoming indicates a new kind, direction or extent of action.

In the evaluation of the conceptual self-relations, the establishment of identity was recognition, in turn, of each of the separate characteristics of self. We cannot know how these characteristics were defined in the self-consciousness of the force, so we must use our own definitions as "something like." They are necessarily analogies.

The new kind of action was the consciousness of differentiation, the new direction was alternation, and the separate concepts of self-being were extended from the single fact of existence. Thus there was a congruent doubling of the self.

When we speak of force of extension, Supra-nature or living spirit we are speaking of one and the same thing but from different viewpoints. There are many nuances we cannot pursue at this time.

Each viewpoint calls for a different definition and different analogies. There are many more labels and viewpoints we could choose, but more would only confuse us further.

We cannot visualize the separation into self-concepts in actuality, we can only say it is something like the force recognizing its own characteristics.

In our view of the advent of these concepts of self as objective power, being and acting, and subjective identity, existence and action, we see the first appearance of the geometric progression of the force's (Creation's) activities.

If we were talking about biology here instead of mentation we would mention something about the division of embryonic cells, each becoming individuated, self-identified, each going forward, continuing on its own.

This analogy is not perfect because the original force continues even as it divides. Biology cannot do this, mentation can.

When we reach this point we find the terms objective and subjective have been well pounded out and no longer exude much meaning for our purpose. Also what is objective to the force is subjective to us, and vice versa, and I have spent many an hour trying to determine which is proper to use in a specific event. It is too confusing.

In any phase of extension, *the tension of equilibrium between the extend directive and the retain directive produces a field upon which the interaction of that phase takes place.* This process is of the utmost importance, as you will discover when we get around to describing true space and true time.

Like a spider spinning a web out of its own body, we can imagine the force of extension as spinning facts of creation out of its own being. It extends self in experience as it retains identity in self-knowledge. The original self endures as the Supra-nature and the immutable laws and potentials of Creation.

Once started, nothing quits. even as it extends itself in myriad ways. Continuation is another principle to always keep in mind. (Until we get to *form* when all sorts of different things happen.)

As the dynamic force of the impulsions extends creation beyond self-concepts only, it lays out a passageway beneath its feet that we call space.

The continued spreading out of space is compressed by the holding back of retention that we call time. Thus their tension of equilibrium becomes a field of spacetime yielding a convoluted effect, which had been seen as potential in the ripples of the field of self-consciousness. (See Figure 5-1.) The ripples in the field of self-consciousness continue and also extend in the field of spacetime. This is the interdimensional or transitional phase between the spiritual and physical. (Elsewhere we have referred to this phase as a psychic area. This perspective is only another way of looking at it, but it is the area in which psychic events become real.)

Time, as the retain directive, coupled with the program of continuation, is transformative. It establishes the *weight of history* in

FIELDS

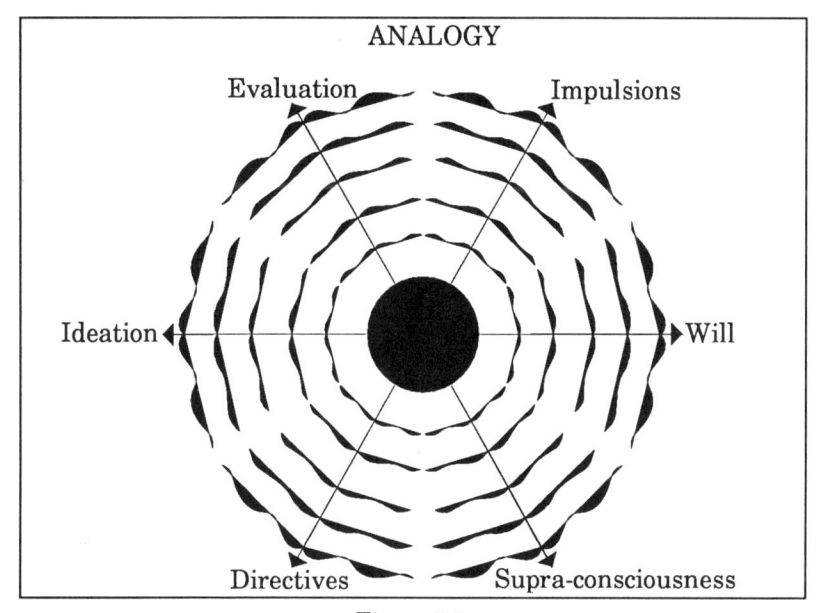

ANALOGY

Evaluation — Impulsions
Ideation ◀——▶ Will
Directives — Supra-consciousness

Figure 5-1
The spreading out of space is compressed by the retention of time.
Concepts emerge as ripples in the field of self-consciousness

any particle, form or object so that *any such object carries within itself the sum total of its life experiences as it has responded to the impulsions of the force.*

There are two extremely vital factors to remember here:
- Space was laid out only as creation extended. It was not pre-existing.
- Time as the retain directive establishes a weight of history in any object. Time retains the life experiences of that object.

Pre-substance is the concept aspect of self-existence. Its area of being and action is the field of consciousness of the Supra-nature. This is the field of the tension of equilibrium of pre-space and pre-time, where these act as a unit and are not observable to us as either space or time. They are still in the spiritual.

Pre-substance can be conceived of, in our closest terms, as pure electricity. Pre-substance would be totally invisible to us, and the ripples we have shown on the diagram would be best described as invisible but potent pulsation.

As the ripples, or concepts, in the field of self-consciousness *resonate* in the extended field of spacetime, the pre-substance extends as a pulsation of spiritual energy translated into the first expectant particles of matter-energy.

A pulsation of spiritual energy that has translated into a quantum of matter-energy *retains* the character of both spiritual and material energy because of the principle of continuation. Because of its antecedents each tiny unit of spiritual-material energy carries within its being a holographic picture (concept) of a universe. It enters the extended world of spacetime already imprinted with intention like a spiritual DNA.

As pre-substance extends into particles of energies, space and time begin to kick each other out as cherished bedfellows. They are imbued with opposing directives or commands, space with the extend command, time with the retain identity command. (See Figure 5-2.)

We can imagine that as the electrical pulsations extend as particles of electrical substance, or matter-energy, that spacetime draws further apart to become space:time and assumes the characteristic of the magnetic forces of attraction and repulsion. With the

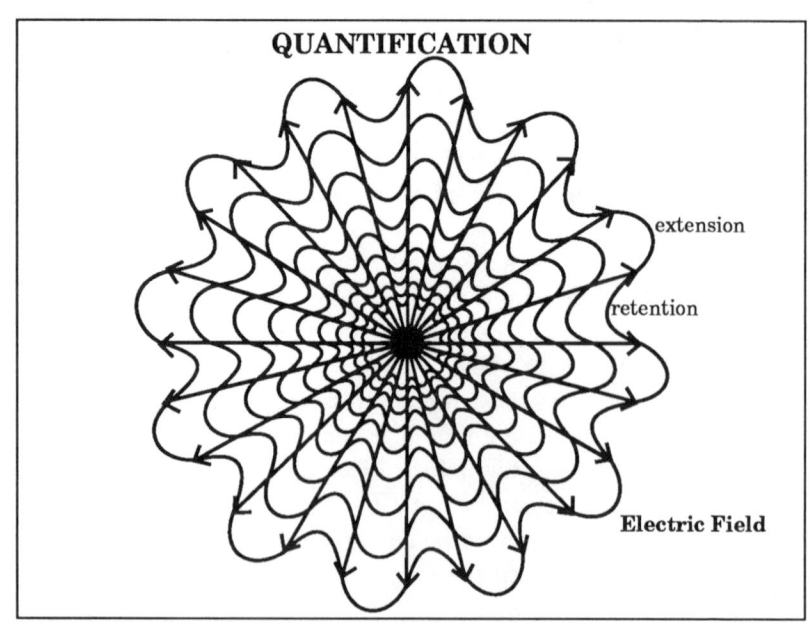

QUANTIFICATION

extension
retention

Electric Field

Figure 5-2.
The force quantifies pre-substance to create particles of positive and negative energies that extend in space and retain in time.

interaction of the positive and negative electric particles the magnetic field produces electromagnetic effects. (See Figure 7-1, p. 53.)

In the next extension space and time are pulled farther apart and are freed of their mutual dependence on each other. They become wholly individual, now able to work in some opposition to each other as space *and* time. The particles extend into new relationships of *form*.

Freed time, imbued with the retain directive, becomes the inertia (weight of history) of the form. Freed space, imbued with the extend directive, becomes a universal gravitational pull. (This force would act very much as anti-gravity in some circumstances.)

The universal gravitational pull and inertia are now able to act in opposition (to some extent) to each other and thereby produce the gravitational field. The observed gravitational and magnetic fields are each the product of transformative time, the retain directive, interacting in a (much extended) tension of equilibrium with space, the extend directive.

The "thrust" that separated the directives, now considered as space and time, was the big bang, described in Chapter 6. It was not until after this event that gravity could come into operation.

In Figure 5-2 we can see that even before advancing space and resistant time entered the material universe they set up a rhythmic or wave-like dynamic.

After their advent into what was to be the four-dimensional physical universe, this dynamic (tension of equilibrium) becomes a universal gravitational pull as space or the extend directive, and inertia as time or the retain directive. The two directives now work freely in opposition to become the gravitational field.

As the universal gravitational pull plays its charm on a particle, electron, molecule or form, it interacts with the resistance mass (inertia) of that object so that it is set into motion of one kind or another. The earth spins as though it can't make up its mind which directive to obey, since both are of equal value. By its spinning (or whatever action) the object demonstrates its inertia and marks out its own gravity field as a resistance or opposition to the universal gravity pull.

Who would believe that inertia is a product of time? If you view it as the retain directive acting upon form it becomes apparent. Or that space provided a gravitational pull? View it as the extend directive and the mystery begins to unravel.

Bringing the formula of extension into the physical universe created many questions of coherence. Without the original "six aspects" given some dialectical identity, I could never have answered these questions, and so the "aspects" became the conceptual self-relations of the Supra-nature. Deciding how to characterize them has been the most difficult chore of this whole study. Their names have changed many times and the final decision has not been a quick or arbitrary one.

Did the full original force act in the physical arena or did only its extended concepts such as space and time act? By referring first to the fully believed concept of continuation (anything once started continues), I decided the original Supra-nature as the full force did indeed interact with the physical. Since all extended existence, including the physical, remains within the being of the self of the Supra-nature, then of course it would interact. Since the full force is the identity of the Supra-nature, and the concept of identity indicates "to be conscious of self-being," the full force is indeed interactive with the physical universe.

How could we as inhabitants of the physical universe recognize the full force? As observers that see individuals of nature reacting to the force, we see only such parts of the force as the individual could utilize. Thus we would recognize many and various "natural forces," not understanding that these were but portions or distinctions of the full force. All the things we call natural forces are just such amounts of the full force of extension that the object we are observing allows to show through.

There is only one master force, Adonai, the living spirit. And over all is the brooding image of God Self: omniscient, omnipresent.

"God sees you. Take your elbows off the table, and don't sass."

CHAPTER

6

True Space And True Time

*I follow you wherever you are from the present hour.
My words itch at your ear till you understand them.*
    Walt Whitman—Song of Myself

When we start to talk about particles and the four-dimensional physical universe in which we live there are several propositions that must be kept in mind and utilized as factors of understanding. I have mentioned some of them before, I will mention them here, and you will meet them again more than once as we progress.
- The tension of equilibrium between the extend and retain commands that sets up fields.
- The directives of the force of extension in equilibrium as the definitions of true space (extend) and true time (retain).
- Time (retain) as the weight of history of an object (inertia).
- Motion: successive change of position of an object in space.
- Each extension is witnessed through a change of motion in kind, direction or extent.
- Continuation of anything once started. (See Figure 6-1.)
- Natural forces as related portions of the full force of extension.
- Substance indicates any existence that may be in some manner observed by us or grasped concretely in our imaginations in its natural properties or character.
- Concepts and concept resonance.

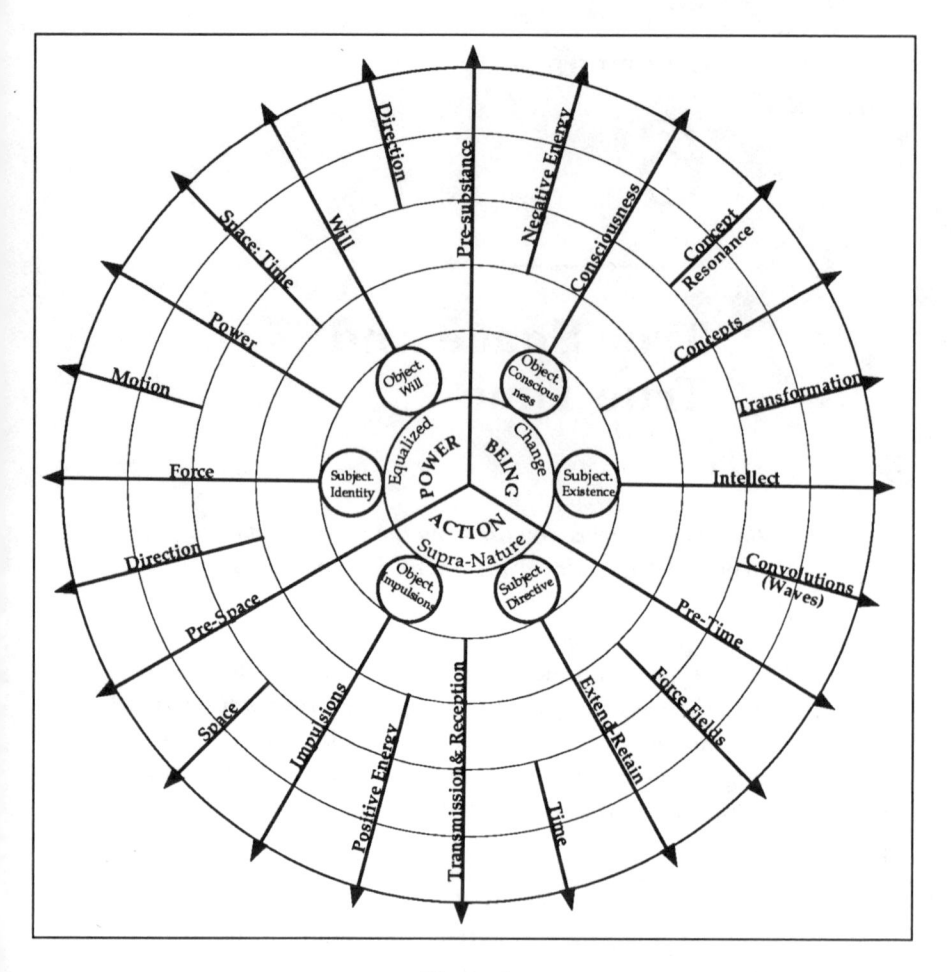

Figure 6-1
Process of Continuation, with geometric progression.
- The directives of space (extend) and time (retain) drawing away from each other: interpenetration, coexistence, coextension, then freed.

Quantum physicists have given us some astounding bits of news about our universe, but there is no logical formula running through their discoveries. They see the universe as a thing of parts, random, scattered, unpredictable and without overall coherence.

Let's pick up a few of those parts and see if we can't glue them all together in some logical coherence.

If we start from the right end of things (creation) and travel in the right direction (evolution), the natural flow of progression will reveal the formula to us.

For years smart people have been telling me there is no such thing as "true" time.

I find true time to be one of the most important things in the physical universe, right alongside of true space. And it is just as dimensional!

So let's start our discussion with time and space, picking them up before the advent of the physical as pre-time and pre-space and flowing onward.

People talk about the three dimensions of space. What they are actually referring to are the three dimensions that objects in space project. Ask them to describe the fourth dimension, time, and they are even more vague. The closest answer I ever received was "age."

Space permits objects situated within it to have three dimensions. But these are actually directions of objects projecting into space.

Consider a typical textbook discussion describing three spatial dimensions. "A current of electric particles traverses a magnetic field at right angles to the flow of the field." This description gives us two directions of measurement. "Both together, as a unit, move at right angles to their separate flows of movement," that is, in a third direction. This points out what we usually call the three dimensions of space. In this case they are directions of movement.

This discussion does not point out the fourth dimension of time, unless you consider the particles' velocities as time. Velocity is measured by the amount of time needed to travel a specific area of space.

So what has all this to do with our discussion? Have we measured or found the true dimensions of space, or just the measurement of something that moves in, through and over space? Space allows this movement and these measurements from this point of view, but the old lady is so much more! Let us give her credit for all her virtues. How shall we introduce her? This is space who sponsors up/down, across and through? Or this is space (extend) who, with her buddy time (retain), has extended universe after universe after universe?

How can that be?

How would you measure or define the dimensions of empty space in which there is absolutely no object of reference, not even its own beginning or end? Where is the beginning or end of space? What shape is space?

We are not trying to prove that space has no dimensions. We are saying that the dimensions of true space are not what we always have thought they were. Moreover we are about to say that true time has as many dimensions as true space. Some of them will knock the socks off you—inertia for one!

Then what is true space and true time? Space is the extend directive in the physical universe as time is the retain directive.

The tension of equilibrium between the two directives sets up a field. Spiritually, this field was the field of consciousness in pre-space and pre-time. The two directives draw further apart in dependency and interaction from interpenetration at the beginning, to coexistence in the interdimensional, to coextension in the physical, and finally to freed space (extend) and freed time (retain). Now the directives are able to work in direct opposition to each other's commands. Each of these four degrees of closeness and interaction creates a different "field," *a different dimension in true space and true time.*

So you see the true dimensions of space and time have nothing to do with height, width, breadth, or velocity, but with fields set up by the tension of equilibrium of the extend and retain directives of the force of extension as the directives work in varying degrees of closeness and interdependency.

Figure 6-2 is a diagram to help keep this in mind. Use it for easy reference any time your mind gets bogged down in my sometimes thick and sticky explanations.

Anything once begun continues, according to our formula, so the spiritual, interdimensional, and physical dimensions all coexist in the same true space and true time.

Don't look *up* for heaven. It is sitting right in the middle of your sofa in that spot you call empty space. And right now!

We will talk more about all this. I just wanted to give you an overview to start with, because the discussion is not always easy to follow. If you have come this far, you are okay; you will make it.

At various times I have tried to present this material in a dozen different ways. Nothing is hasty. Perhaps I have belabored it overlong and have beaten it dry. I will try to be more relaxed in my

Directives as Space and Time
INTERPENETRATIVE
Pre-space   **Pre-Time**

Concepts   Supra-nature

SPIRITUAL

Field of Consciousness

Concept Resonance   *New individuation set free*

Pulses of spiritual energy   Coexistent SpaceTime   Particles of matter-energy

INTERDIMENSIONAL

Electric Field (nonmagnetic)

Quarks and Leptons   *New individuation set free*

Electric particles   Coextensive Space:Time   Magnetic energies

Magnetic Field

Form Electromagnetic Effects   *New individuation set free*

PHYSICAL

Freed Space   Freed Time in opposition

Gravitational Field

Extension of space yields universal gravitational pull   Retention of time yields inertia

Gravitational Effects

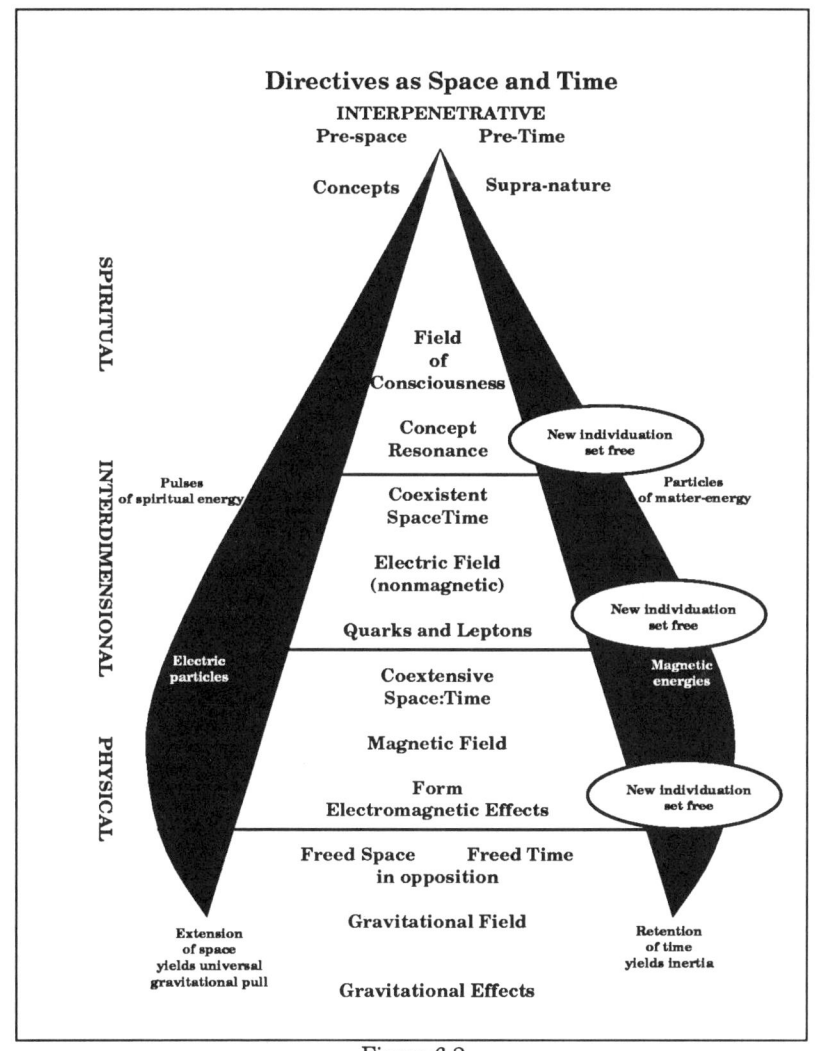

Figure 6-2
Space extends to create the universal gravitational pull, while time retains the weight of history as inertia.

presentation. On the other hand, I do not want to obscure with silly sentences information I think is important. Please bear with me.

Our table gives us a unified field theory. Our four fields continue always in geometric relationship to each other.

We are giving the advent of the physical dimension in some detail, hoping it will make the subsequent material seem more real and more down to earth. The geometries of the formula are dreadfully hard to convey all at one time. We can only offer them in layers and hope the interaction and relationships will show up themselves. As portrayed, each of the layers (dimensions) underlie the others like the layers of a cake, with the force of extension running between and topping them all. (See Figure 6-3.)

```
FORCE ──┬── Supra-nature
        ├── Interdimensional
        ├── Physical Particles
        └── Physical Form
```

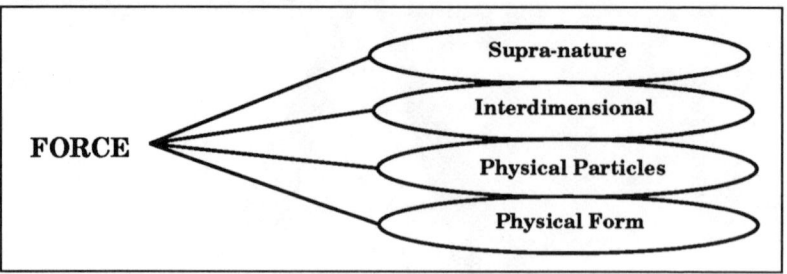

Figure 6-3
The Four Dimensions of Space and Time

In his book, *The Music of the Spheres*, Guy Murchie remarks: "In fact space turns out to have a kind of geometric 'pressure pattern' that is invisible, impalpable, immensely subtle, and the very devil to keep track of."

I'm sure we know exactly what he means!

While there is interaction between all the layers of our cake, the instructions flow in one direction only. "Keep moving," says space. "You can't go back," says time.

The Supra-nature instructs the interdimensional and the physical layers. The interdimensional layer informs the physical layers, but the physical layers do not instruct the Interdimensional or the Supra-nature layers.

Once my hidden voices told me that they occupied the same space as myself but in a different time dimension. Our four-dimensional layer cake illustrates what this means. The Hidden One is from the Interdimensional layer and he has told me that his "body" is almost pure energy, that is, electricity. He has said that if my psychic abilities were really awake, I would be able to enter his world but with the requisite that I leave behind the "weight of history" of my physical self and bring along only my "identity" self (my dopple gänger). I refer to such a visit as an out-of-body experience. I am just now beginning to realize how this fits into the pattern of reference (formula) we are outlining here.

Particles provide limitations and opportunities to the *form*. Form does not remake the particles.

This prohibition repeats the injunction that each factor in the universe retains its identity and also continues once started. By these rules everything in the universe *evolves*. By the same rules, the universe becomes ever more complex, and its factors do not converge into some kind of homogeneous sludge, that is, not after space has once been laid out and gravity and spin emerged.

Each factor retains its individual character. Particles do not lose their identity when they collaborate into form. These principles have great bearing on our personal lives, as we shall see presently.

One form can change another form readily enough, at least insofar as our observation goes, but not the basic particles. A quark is a quark is a quark. (I think someone said that but I can't remember whom to credit.)

Particles may be coerced into form through means of collaborative relationships, but they retain their identity. Form may be broken down into particles, sometimes with great difficulty. The more basic the form, the greater is the difficulty. Entropy and decay may break down the more elaborate forms.

Space and time as freed and opposing directives involve the process of entropy and decay. These include the redistribution of materiality when form separates back into particles. *But*—these particles are different than when they started! They have been transformed by their weight of history (experience and time). Therefore the changes of decay and entropy are still a process of evolution as new kinds of *experienced* particles are born (extended). *Nothing goes back unchanged!*

As for the cosmological viewpoint of the universe, what is to prevent our imaginations from adopting both the steady-state creation and the Big Bang?

What happened before the Big Bang? Where did all that material that was thrown out come from?

From the steady state that preceded it. Matter was created in the steady state mode as *space first extended with it*. This meant that the material cohered into a single mass. There was not empty space to spread out in, matter was involving space as it went. There was not yet the spin of gravity to release friction. The mass grew more packed, denser and hotter until critical mass was reached, and the Big Bang occurred. Did someone make a mistake?

No, it was just the formula of extension fulfilling itself. Each new extension occurs through a change in kind, direction or extent of motion.

The Big Bang definitely was a change of motion in every possible factor, and a rather decisive one. Even extension of the impulsions, as a kind of radiation, was included.

We would like to call attention to the fact that the spiritual and interdimensional (or *psychic*) worlds are totally different areas, different universes. My hidden friends have often exclaimed over the way we confuse the two.

It has also been called to our attention that the interdimensional or psychic world is *real* and our psychic experiences are not the result of mental aberrations or incompetency. "They" also dislike the word "paranormal."

"Your psychic abilities are absolutely normal and should be accepted, studied and used properly."

But the word that makes them shudder above all is "occult." They call it a degrading term leading to evil practices.

CHAPTER

7

Waves

*It is not chaos or death—it is form, union, plan,
it is eternal life—it is Happiness.*
                      Walt Whitman—*Song of Myself*

The first moments of pre-substance, which have differentiated into the pulsations of spiritual energy, release pre-space and pre-time into spacetime so that the directives are able to act coexistently rather that interpenetratively, thus with a little more independence of each other. The impulsions of pre-space and pre-time continue according to the demands of the formula, even as spacetime comes into action.

The moment of quantification is scarcely more than a slight pulsation, a *concept resonance*, like an electric spark in the fabric of pre-substance, a translation of the Supra-nature. The exertion of the retain (time) directive does not allow the pulsations to return unchanged to their source, but they extend, transformed, as the first particles of matter-energy, retaining their spiritual energy as well.

The pulsation extends and retains, extends and retains, setting up a wave motion into expanding space. (Refer back to Figure 5-2 on page 40.) The moment of pulsation is not random, but it is unpredictable to an "observer," because he does not see the force and the events that promoted it.

The moment occurs when the history according to the force of extension has prepared it to do so. The history would appear as chaos to our noncomprehension.

The apparent spontaneity of this event is not without law and order, as is witnessed by our description of all that led up to this event.

Chaos and random events are misconceptions of those who believe that Creation started at this moment and do not see all that went before. The "all that went before" is what we have tried to discover in this writing up to this point.

We have thus discovered the principle of extension in the force's self-translation of its spiritual nature into pulsations and the transformation of the pre-substance into particularized quanta of positive and negative character. We must recall the principle of retention and realize that because of this principle the quanta inherits spiritual energies as well, thus the Supra-nature "retains" itself even in this extension. Our tiny little particle of matter is truly a vehicle of the spiritual. Will we ever be able to observe this spiritual component? Probably not, but in our imaginations we have observed how all this came about and that it is so.

In this total event we have seen energies translated, existence transformed and action released into our observable area.

Might we glimpse here the idea that the seemingly conflicting doctrines of creationism and evolution are both true and coexistent, two sides of a coin? Both of these concepts can be encompassed in one phrase: "extension—the becoming."

Once the particles have been set free, spacetime releases its grip on its two components, which now become observable as space:time. The dynamic interaction of space:time plus the impulsions of the free force become what we would call a magnetic field.

To the new electric particles, this space:time field offers magnetic properties of attraction and repulsion. At this point space and time are coextensive, still connected, but pulling against each other like a pair of stubborn mules wanting to do opposite things, but unable either to let go or to give in.

In order for the quantized particles of positive and negative energies to interact with the magnetic field, they must act alternately as independent or individuated particles, so a wave process is set up within the field correspondent to the wave process of the electric, or nonmagnetic, field. These two fields appear opposing, like mirror images to each other. (See Figure 7-1.)

The particles reacting to this magnetic field begin to gather together, to swirl about and form new relationships in their next extension into form. Electromagnetic effects are now observable. Space:time next extends again into freed space and freed time, appearing not only as individuals, but able to work independently of

WAVES

MAGNETIC FIELD

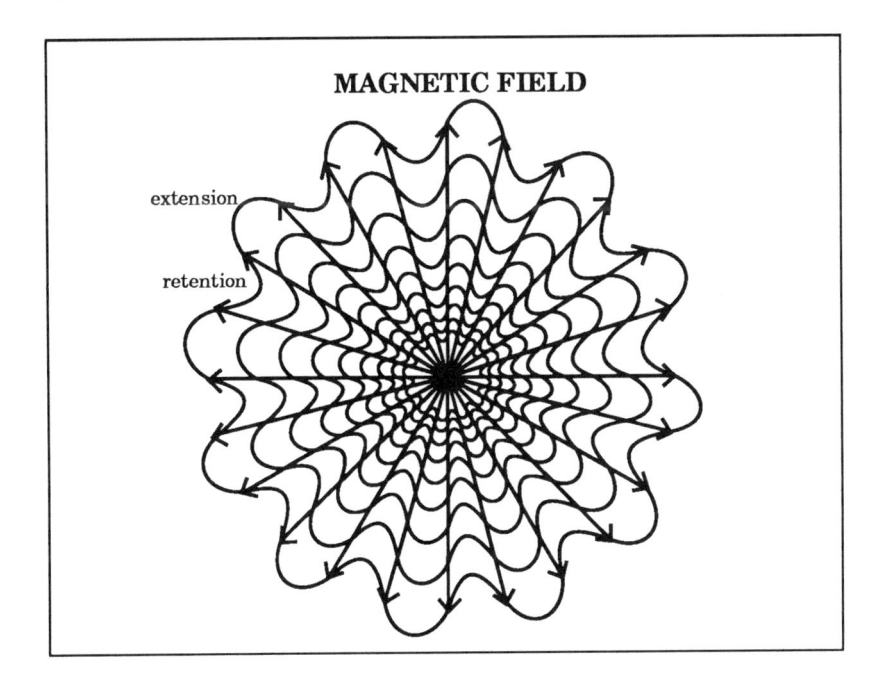

extension

retention

Figure 7-1
The Magnetic Field is a mirror image of the electric field, where space extends and time retains in the convolutions of space:time.

each other, and even in direct opposition. They never entirely lose touch, or the tension of equilibrium would be broken.

Freed space would become observable as a Universal Gravitational Pull and freed time would become observable as inertia, the weight of history in an object.

The field–tension of equilibrium–set up between freed space and freed time (as universal gravitational pull and inertia) would be the gravitational field.

If this development seems difficult to follow, compare it to yourself and your self's varied phases as a person. A man is a son, a husband or a father. Does any one of these life phases prohibit him from being any of the others? No, he is his own self in each and all of them, and retains his personal identity in each and all. He is all of them at once.

These vitally important things we call space and time have many phases and appear differently in each, sometimes unrecognizably.

If we seem to be repeating ourselves over and over in some of these propositions, it is because they are so important for one thing, and then each presentation is in a slightly different context. Only in this way can we ever hope to keep up with the geometrical complexities of the facts. We are not redundant, we are only repetitive!

In any phase the tension of equilibrium between the extend directive and the retain directive produces a field upon which the interaction of that phase takes place. To exemplify, let us choose a phase in which the interaction is easiest to follow:

Let us observe a particle sitting happy as a duck in the middle of his field and observe his reactions and interactions with that field. Only by seeing this interaction can we see how a wave action appears and why the wave is not a "thing" itself, but a process more apparent than actually real.

The particle does not set up his field. The field is a communal affair of whatever aspect of space and time (extend and retain) is in phase for that particular type of particle. The field is the current manifestation of the directives of the force of extension to extend and retain *its own self*.

The activity of the particle is measured by its possibilities according to its nature, or energy potential, but *the impetus and concept of the possibility and desirability of action comes from its place in the specific community of nature surrounding it, i.e. its field.*

We are inclined to say that a particle is a unit of energy. We should say, more exactly, that because of its nature, a particle is able to receive the concept of energy expenditure from the force field and to exhibit that concept in a burst of action. Its inherent energetic nature resonates with the calling of the directives. After this burst of energy it relaxes momentarily as it has a transformative time experience before its next active space experience. It is adding to its weight of history, and we call this its inertia.

The directives (extend and retain), the field of space and time in the proper phase, and the particle are all working in a partnership to produce the result or effect. *The particle does not create its field. Its activity reveals as much of the communal field as it is able to use, to call its own for the period of time it is needed.*

The alternate burst of energy and the interval of time of relaxation produces what appears to be a wave, or a wave effect. The wave is an appearance, a process, not an actual thing. It cannot extend itself to act as a free thing on its own. It only becomes apparent in the presence of particles, as the particles interact with the field.

The weight of history of a particle (or form which is a composite of many particles) is the sum total of all its retain (time) experiences.

There is something that must be carefully clarified here or we will be leading you astray. Let us consider how light can be both a particle and a wave, i.e., how a particle of light, a photon, can act in a wavelike process.

If we think of the photon as starting at the light source and hurling itself with incredible speed at our eyeball it would be very difficult to explain the wave process. But how about this scenario? Our photon stays strictly at home, cozy in his own place, and lets some of his brethren help with the work. They each, in resonance, pass a burst of energy, like a bucket brigade down the incredibly crowded avenues of space. Between each photon's burst is a time interval (retain) with the resulting appearance of a wave that stands at right angles to the direction of propagation.

If the photon itself traveled at that speed it would pierce your retina instead of the latest squad of photons merely imprinting an image or sensation on it. If the photon were traveling and hit an obstacle, it would splash. A resonance between photons would merely stop.

The wave *motion* is transferred as excitation of energy from photon to photon, the photons themselves do not travel. If you concentrate your attention on one photon you "freeze" the observation of the motion and therefore cannot see the transfer of energy—the wave motion—the relationship of action between photons.

The same rules apply to any other type of particle as it interacts in whatever field is in phase to its nature, the electric particle interacting with the magnetic field, or an electromagnetic particle interacting with the gravitational-field. If my explanation sounds a little dense, remember our definition of motion—motion itself is only apparent, as a body (or particle) changes position in space. In this case the change of position is an expenditure of energy.

A field is naturally created by the tension of equilibrium of space (extend) and time (retain) in their various phases. Therefore there can be no particle of a field. A field is nonparticulate. It is coherent. If it were particulate, the tension would break, and there would be no field.

Space (extend) and time (retain) come in phases. Each phase is characterized by the two drawing ever further apart in action and dependency. In pre-time and pre-space they are interpenetrative; in spacetime they are coexistent; in space:time they are coextensive, and in freed space and freed time they may work in opposition.

A field is sensitized and reactive, it pulses and inspires, because it is actually the extend-retain impulsions of the force of extension as space and time.

There are no gravitons. There is no electromagnetic field. The magnetic field is the product of space:time as coextensive directives. Electric particles interacting with the magnetic field produce electromagnetic effects.

The gravitational field is produced by the interaction of the universal gravitational pull, which is space (extend) versus inertia, which is time (retain) in its aspect of the weight of history of an object.

Let us summarize:
- The tension of equilibrium of pre-space and pre-time produces the field of consciousness (intellect or pre-substance) of the Supra-nature.
- In the interdimensional layer, spacetime produces the field of electricity, or nonmagnetic field. (In some instances this field acts as antimagnetic field.)
- Space:time produce the magnetic field.
- Freed space (universal gravitational pull) and freed time (inertia) produce the gravitational field.

I know I keep saying this over and over and I am not through yet!

There are answers to hundreds of questions and mysteries hidden in the propositions we have examined up to now. It would take ten lifetimes to explore them all. Let us consider some of the unanswered questions of the physicists:

David Bohm's neorealist quantum theory was based upon a model recognizing ordinary objects (so the books tell me), but he needed to prove that every object was in some way in instant contact with every other object in the world. With the force of extension and the fields marked out by the activities of the directives, everything in the world is so connected. He also needed something that traveled at superluminal speeds. Impulsions do.

I have read that the four great forces of nature are carried by neither a particle nor a field, but by something that partakes of both. (Force of extension and impulsions).

I read also that if John Bell's theorem is correct, then invisible nonlocal connections must truly exist—the force of extension and impulsions again!

The influence of the force of extension and its impulsions is everywhere all the time, therefore certainly nonlocal. Since, as pure impulsions, they are still in the interdimensional layer, they have neither mass nor inertia nor any physical drag that forbids them superluminal speed. They are as pervasive and instantaneous as thoughts in a mind. They are concepts and extend in the four-dimensional world in concept resonance. So thoughts in a mind they really are, but not my mind, nor yours, nor the quantum physicists.

God exists in every particle of your being. Be respectful.

CHAPTER

8

Identity

And I have dreamed that the purpose and essence of the known life, the transient, is to form and decide identity for the unknown life, the permanent.
           Walt Whitman—*To Think of Time*

Let us turn our thoughts about and look at the process from the viewpoint of extended things, such as ourselves. The weight of history of the form is the recapitulation of its evolution, like the DNA code. As such, it has been the inheritance of being of each individual of the form, to which each individual adds its own attempts at extension. First comes individuation, then form, then individuals of the form. The continuation of the form is the basic security level of the individual, so that the larger energies of the individual of that form may be directed toward avenues of self-extension in collaboration with the force.

In that the force itself, in its phase of self-becoming, encompasses pure intellect, or absolute consciousness it does not need intellectual faculties. In its primal state the force exists in an atmosphere of eternal being. It is outside of time. Even as it continues forever, the force is still outside of our conventional time measurements, existing concurrently to them but not of them. Therefore, from its own viewpoint, there is no "past" requiring memory, no "future" requiring foresight, and nothing existing outside of its own existence requiring imagination.

But it is through such faculties as imagination, foresight, and judgment predicated upon memory that man, as mind thinking in the framework of space and time, serves as an extension of the pure intellect of the primal force. If the force had such faculties, man could not have them, but would have something else extended from them. Man can extend his mind, thoughts or ideas according to his nature, or he can distort them from extension into futile avenues. He can imagine or fancy what does not exist. Man's thoughts and imaginings are the only things in the universe which can be false. All other things exist in the truth of their own nature, without the necessity of discovering that truth. Man's imagination can also help him discover further truths outside of his own nature.

The impulsions by which the force of extension compels a thing to extend are something we cannot visualize exactly. A force is intangible. It cannot be seen. These impulsions of power:being:acting while extending from the absolute reality can only be imagined as "something like" something we already know.

The impulsions are something like a perpetual radiation, or vibration, or a concentric pressure, or lines of stress. They are absolutely changeless, absolutely always, and absolutely everywhere, both inside and outside the identity that is experiencing them.

In humanistic terms, Thomas Merton (Trappist monk 1915-1968) would have called the impulsions the all-pervading love of God. They are life. Life is not something that is produced by the pounding heart and the breathing lungs of an organism. Rather, life is what compels the heart to beat and the lungs to breathe. Merton said, "Were this life, this all-pervading love of God to withhold its self for even one instant, all living things would die and all created things would fall apart." It is quite conceivable that science some day will create a mechanism so properly responsive to the impulsions of the living force that science will absurdly declare it has created life.

If our own individuated identity comes into the reality of being that was intended for it by its inheritance of human form, and it further strives to complete that reality according to the historical pattern of development bequeathed to it, the individuated identity will, at the seeming death of the body, come into extended life. This is as close as individuated identity can come to eternal life, since it has not had conscious identity since the beginning.

When the impulsions first extend through any individuation, compelling the individuation's first act of extension, this new individuation, which up to then was a dissociated concept of relation, now becomes concretized in factual being, and it comes into its own identity.

The primal force, as Supra-nature, obtains knowledge or evaluation of individuated identities such as ourselves, in its process of using them for further extensions of itself. We, as individuated identities, do not partake as extensions of the concept of primary self-relations, or the concretized selves, but as concepts of relations extended into space and time. Such concepts become concretized in us as individuated identities with quantitative being (individuals of the translation into form—bodies) and qualitative being (transformations of life within the individuals of the form). But in some way, we do exist as concepts of extended relations, in the pre-space (consciousness) of the Supra-nature before we become concretized through evaluation as individual identities in what to us is "actual existence" in space and time.

The thread of cohesion that runs through every being, every existence in the universe and holds it together as "a thing in itself" is the identity of the force's self, i.e., it is the force's act of consciousness or recognition of self-being in the individuated things. The problems of evil and disease appear when the impulsions of the force are received and acted upon as though they originated in the form itself, i.e., action chosen on the basis of the self will of the form, and without possibility of collaboration with the force.

It is an error to say that the opposite of life is death. The opposite of life is nonidentity. What we call death is identity set free of time and space relationships. It is not dispersed back into the absolute, but having been once extended and "known" as individuated identity, it forever continues as such.

We must recall that the force did not create the universe as something outside itself. The universe is the force extended within its own being, not by adding new substances or energies to primal existence, but by liberating or dissociating concepts or setting free new manifestations of itself. From its own viewpoint, all this extension is a continuity of self in identity and being, as force, not as persons. But from our individuated viewpoint in space and time, each new manifested thing or identity appears as a discontinuity—a new individuated identity. It is this seeming discontinuity, involving a new translation of identity, which is the natural freedom of the identity to exist according to its own nature. It is its freedom to come into realization of individuated identity, to have its own personal experience, to exercise free will and to suffer profit or loss (reward or punishment) thereby, extending itself.

As long as a man lives alone, it is enough that he be rational enough to come in out of the rain, but when he comes into contact with his fellows, rational living is not enough—he must also be moral. Men without moral honor would have remained isolated from each other or at best run in small predatory packs like wolves, like the Dalton gang or the Younger boys.

It is not only our human moral obligation, but also our spiritual necessity that we establish, maintain and develop our identities according to the pattern of the human form and in such a way that we collaborate with the force of extension. On it rests not only our temporal health, well-being and happiness, but also our estate after death.

Individual "mind" recognizes individual identity. Mind does not create identity and is not synonymous to it. Identity is, in some way, more nearly correlative to "will," the will "accepts" it.

Neither are intellect and will synonymous, but collaborate with and counterbalance each other, making temporal life and spiritual life concurrently possible.

The general purpose of man is the same as for all created or "extended" things—to collaborate in the self-extension of the living force (Supra-nature). But specifically and from humanity's own viewpoint in space and time, his reason for being, his purpose, is to extend the consciousness of the force. It is not to extend new ideas about the force in man's consciousness, but to extend the force's consciousness of itself in individuated identities and experiences.

CHAPTER

9

Extension in Space and Time

Now understand me well—it is provided in the essence of things that from any fruition of success, no matter what, shall come forth something to make a greater struggle necessary.
    Walt Whitman—*Song of the Open Road*

A frequent and recurring feeling is that life as we observe it is not real life at all, but only a reflection of life as it is actually being lived somewhere else in the universe. Perhaps this feeling occurs because what is actually occurring within a form can be understood only from the viewpoint of the force, while what we see from our individuated viewpoint is a kind of mirror reflection or backward viewpoint of the actuality. When we try to observe the reality of the thing through this mirror, we do not grasp its reality, nor can we understand "how it got that way."

It is difficult to pin down the phases of self-creation and extension of the force, for there are no phases actually bracketed off as phases of becoming, but only phases of observation as we make them up or imagine them in order to catch hold of the continuous action long enough to think about it from some viewpoint and to describe it as best we may. That is to say, from the viewpoint of the acting force, the action is continuous; from the viewpoint of individuated things, we see the discontinuous result of the action as individuated things and experiences. In order to really comprehend what it is we are observing, we must try to see it from two opposite viewpoints at once, and to see it as a continuous thing from one viewpoint even as we understand how it appears as a discontinuity from the other.

It is sometimes useful to give an analogy so that the imagination may have something concrete to hang onto, or the abstract idea will evaporate as mist before it can be adequately scrutinized. However, analogies are to be used sparingly, for they can be dangerous. Carried beyond the bare limits of statement or carried to an unwarranted extreme, they carry our fancies over the abyss, and suddenly to our horror the concept that we are considering shatters and falls to nothingness, and we hear our own voices babbling frantically about something of which we have not the slightest knowledge or understanding.

No sooner is an individuation manifested than the force compels it to extend itself. This is the immutable law. The prior individuation continues even as the new one extends itself, and before we can pin this process down to examine it, the next individuation has extended, and another is extending from it.

Because of difficulties such as these, when we try to be both lucid and exact we find it advisable to keep a tight rein on our enthusiasm and to proceed with a necessary but truly exasperating caution in making declarations and drawing conclusions.

From the viewpoint of the force, there are four degrees of becoming:
- *conceptual,* when a thing is potential
- *substantial,* when it is being extended
- *activated,* when it has been extended and is extending itself, and
- *concrete,* when it continues even as a new individuation extended from it's extending Self. We say that this evaluation by the force concretizes identity. An individual identity is not an absolute reality but a concrete reality.

We do not say that the force has a soul. As subjective reality, it is spirit. Nor do we say it has a mind. As objective reality, it is Supra-consciousness. The force is Conscious Spirit, or Knowing Spirit. We do not say it is All-Soul, for that would only be a summation of all individuated souls. Nor do we say it is All-Mind or All-Consciousness, for it is infinitely and eternally more than that. It is Conscious Spirit, and what it is conscious of is its own infinite and eternal existence, self-becoming and extension in space and time in and through all individuated things. We should not say that "the unisphere taken as a whole" is the force, for the force is itself,

self-existent as Supra-nature, self-becoming as Conscious Spirit, plus everything in the unisphere as extended from itself.

We refer to the *unisphere* rather than a universe, to denote that all extended things are held within the being of the force. It denotes a sphere of influence. This is not to suggest a particular shape, the shape could be anything, actually it is probably no constant shape at all. A good diagrammatic way of visualizing the self-becoming of the force would be as two equilateral pyramids, intersecting at right angles and interpenetrative at the apex (Supranature). This is not the shape of the unisphere or a picture of the force —it is a diagram of the interrelationships of self-becoming. (See Figure 9-1.)

A more esoteric interpretation of the diagram has been offered by my "alien" contacts—a triangle with the point down sym-

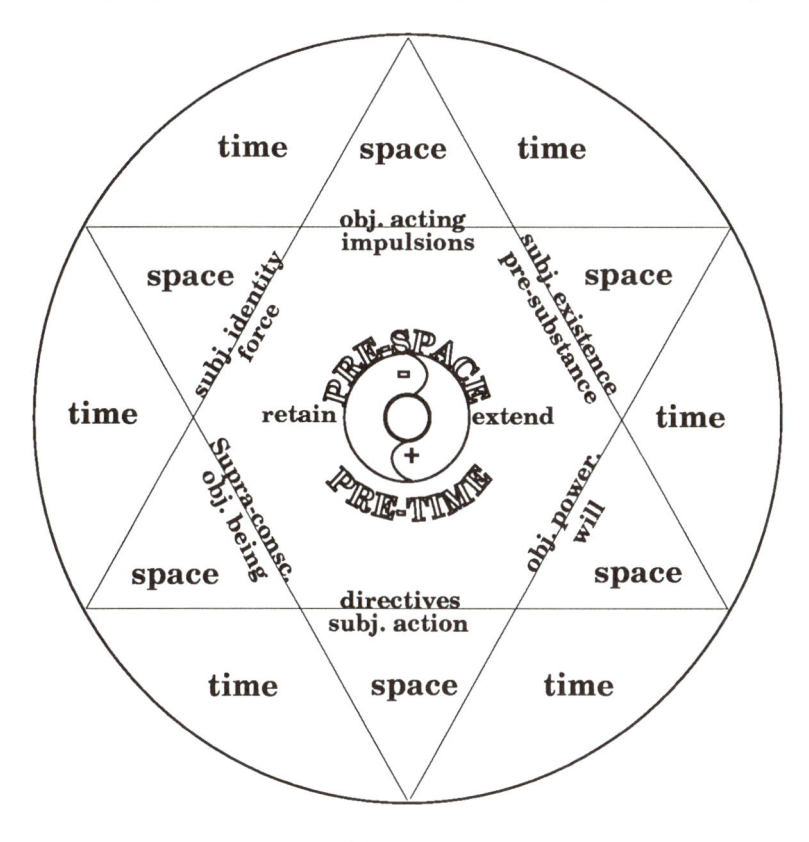

Figure 9-1
The Interrelationships of Self-becoming

bolizes from heaven to earth. The one with the point up symbolizes from earth to heaven. When they are intertwined, they represent heaven and earth in collaboration.

Diagrams are particularly useful in establishing relationships between various factors of an idea. Like the atomic table, they help us to realize missing parts and to estimate probabilities. In themselves symbols and diagrams have no validity, reality or value. They are helpful as reminders, as a kind of short-hand memory. They must not be taken for magic talismans nor for the be-all and end-all of an idea.

This figure is recognized in both Hindu and Chaldean-Jewish cosmogonies and in various societies, but the published interpretations are even more absurd than our own.

With extension in space and time the force is passing always into greater and greater diversifications, but the diversification is of its own being, power in action, experience and self knowledge. It is not at all relative to nor necessarily apparent to individuated identities in space and time. We must reluctantly abandon the notion or hope that the unisphere was created for our good or that the force made the world for our pleasure. It made both the unisphere and us from its own extension of being, and we must learn the system of resolving our problems within that necessity.

God as Supra-nature is Conscious Spirit. Man is spiritual consciousness, or soul, plus a spiritual reality that is God's viewpoint through the particular individual of experience and being in space and time.

That which seems most "real" to us is what we experience through our senses, but what would seem most "real" to the force would be things of nonmaterial and intangible being, spiritual realities. Therefore, when the force, as Supra-nature, dissociates self into conceptual self relations, it extends itself into very real creations of self-being, though nonmaterial.

In phase two the force acting upon "existence" extends self into the elemental particles of substance. The force acting upon self as "being" extends self into purely spiritual individual existences (we can imagine the potential of souls and angels here. See Figure 9-2.)

Quantified particles in space:time would appear to the force itself as moments of self-experienced (known) in durations of extension with intervals of retention and with further sequences of extension-retention since an action once begun continues. The new

EXTENSION IN SPACE AND TIME

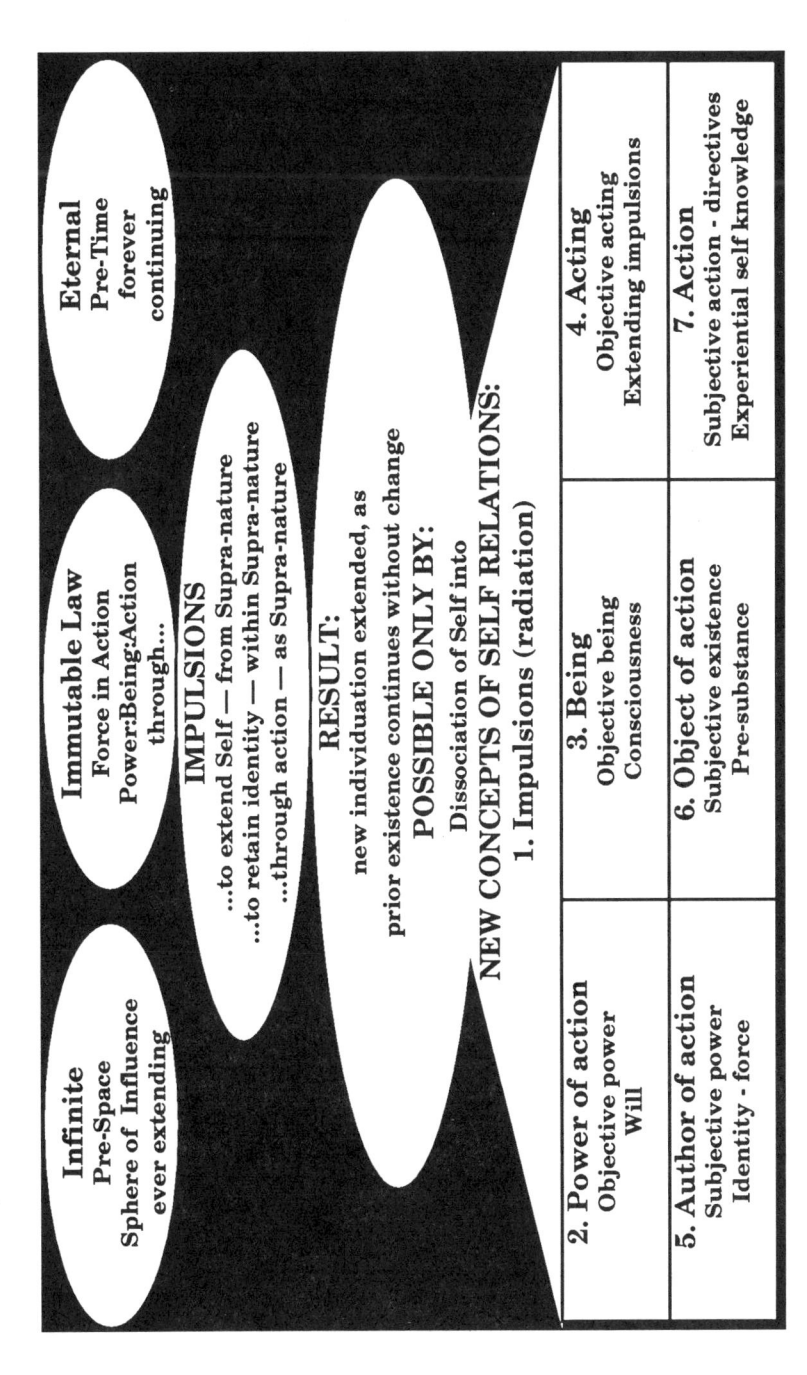

Infinite
Pre-Space
Sphere of Influence
ever extending

Immutable Law
Force in Action
Power:Being:Action
through...

Eternal
Pre-Time
forever continuing

IMPULSIONS
...to extend Self — from Supra-nature
...to retain identity — within Supra-nature
...through action — as Supra-nature

RESULT:
new individuation extended, as
prior existence continues without change
POSSIBLE ONLY BY:
Dissociation of Self into
NEW CONCEPTS OF SELF RELATIONS:
1. Impulsions (radiation)

2. Power of action Objective power Will	3. Being Objective being Consciousness	4. Acting Objective acting Extending impulsions
5. Author of action Subjective power Identity - force	6. Object of action Subjective existence Pre-substance	7. Action Subjective action - directives Experiential self knowledge

Figure 9-2: Extending into Substantial Existence

concept of self-being in this phase is in alternation of the directives rather than co-extensive and contingent in spacetime or co-existent and interpenetrative in pre-space and pre-time. Alternation sets free motion with the potential of directional motion in the next phase.

From the viewpoint of individuated things such as we, these occasions or moments appear as particles of something, a substance having both a positive and negative nature. Its *negative* (physical) *nature* is indicated in the way in which it could be acted upon and its *positive* (physical) *nature* is indicated by how it could act (self-directed motion), depending on whatever weight of history it carries within its being, its inheritance, or "physical" nature.

We would have no clue that it also has a spiritual nature, and we would find that nature difficult to imagine. However, as it is a moment of extension of the pre-substance (consciousness) of the force, it would have a spiritual nature as well. It comes into its own identity as an extended thing. As we prod, pry and peer, we see that the one fact of its nature that reveals to us its spiritual reality is its absolute indestructibility. It is so elemental a stuff that it cannot be broken down to further elements. It is so submaterial that it cannot be sliced with a scalpel. It is so elusive and transparent that it cannot be held under a microscope. At the same time, it is so close to absolute reality that it cannot be left out of accounting, or else nothing in extended nature can be adequately explained. We can only imagine what it must be and how it must act, using ideas deduced from the principles and materials already noted. We must try to bring it down to some point of possibility to see if our imaginings match any known facts.

All natural things in the unisphere contain four dimensions of being:
- quantitative self
- qualitative identity or characteristics,
- its sensitive apparatus, which allows it to respond to the force, and to extend self, which is its spiritual reality within space and time, its psyche or soul reality, and
- its larger spiritual reality, which is actually its evaluation (recognition) by the force, its fourth dimension of being.

From our viewpoint, the nature of these particles of substance, as something that acts, have a positive quotient. As something that may be acted upon, the particles have a negative quotient. Space is not simply a void filled up with particles of something behaving in a certain way, but space itself is a field of action in which the field contributes to or participates in the kind of action. The force field serves as an impenetrable barrier so that the moments once concretized (evaluated in their own action) as particles cannot again return to or dissolve back into the spiritual area of pre-space.

In Figures 5-2 and 7-1 (advancing space and resistant time), we see that even before space and time entered our four-dimensional universe they had set up a rhythmic or wave-like dynamic.

After space and time emerged, individually distinguishable into what was to become the material four-dimensional universe, their rhythmic or wavelike dynamic became a universal gravitational field that acts upon all mass (particles, bodies, entities, objects) in the four-dimensional universe.

The command of the force of extension to extend became, in this phase, the universal gravitational pull, while the command to retain became the resistance of the mass upon which the extend command subsequently acts. Each command is of equal value. The resistance of the mass coheres matter.

As matter is born as particles, we see that all changes made within natural matter are made through motion of particles, from the smallest to the most complex, from quanta to molecules. Motion denotes successive changes of position in space.

Space is the sphere of influence of the *extensions* of the force and as the sphere of "that which is extending" only, it does not permit the particles of substance to return to their former states. From the viewpoint of individuated things, space serves as a barrier or field that institutes *direction* and guarantees *indestructibility* of these elements of substantial being or substance.

Time is the sphere of influence of the *retention* of the force. It is the effort to "retain the identity" of the force. It retains that which was extended in space in an effort to draw all new individuation back to the self, but also to allow individuals to retain their own identities and to exist as experiential knowledge of self within the being of the force. It guarantees indestructibility of identity. Time releases directional motion. The particles reveal the successive change of position, as bodies in space, which is directional motion.

Space allows quantitative translation, extension through dissociation and new relationships. Time allows qualitative transformation, extension through the individual holding within itself its weight of history, the experience of which contributes to the growth and development of the individual.

Time does not allow individuation to return unchanged. Space does not permit the extended particles to remain static, but urges them into action or experience at a velocity (an ardor and endurance) dependent on their inherent nature, their weight of history. The actual duration of a thing is relative to its velocity of change of relationships (directional motion). From our individuated viewpoint we observe the area of change of relationships as form, the outline of motion within the cohesion of identity. In effect time says, "You can't go back." Space says, "You must keep moving." In this action a pattern is traced of every action that ever was. There is no way to erase the record, the result or pattern of an experience once it is known.

The positive quotient is dependent on the way in which a thing extends itself, its potential of extension, a new kind of action. The positive quotient in our substance particles is observable in the potential of directional motion of the particles, by which, in phase three, the particles partake of new relationships with other individuated particles and establishes forms of subatomic structures.

From the viewpoint of the force, the spiritual reality depends on the way the individuated particles serve as an extension of the force. It is noted through a new kind of self-experience. The force experiences (or knows) itself as substance or as substantial being. From our viewpoint, the indestructibility of the substance particles is their evidence of spiritual reality.

That which is farthest from the primal force in extension carries the most weight of history within its materiality. The more times its components of self have responded as materiality to the force, and the more sensitized it has become through its material being, the more self-conscious or sensitive to God, it is. Drawing farther away in materiality, it comes closer in individuated spiritual realization and consciousness. Recalling that to God the most real things are spiritual rather than material, we see that we are actually drawing closer to Him, but in our own individuated identity. It is in no sense a return to an original state, rather a drawing close in our own identities.

Form is the outline of motion within the cohesion of identity. The new relationships of particles in phase three indicated directional motion in space and cohesion, but never interpenetration of individuated particles. Form is an extension of the force in space. It involves a quantitative translation of force into individuated identities, which thereafter, in phase four, develop qualitatively in time, in transformation within identity (personal character).

Cohesion indicates how a group of particles acts in a relationship or an organized or "social" form of identity. The individual identity of the particle is not destroyed nor interpenetrated, but it is increased in power by acting as part of a greater whole. In order to do so, the particle gives up some of its independence, some of its more wildly abandoned, useless actions, in order to cooperate in more purposeful or serviceable action with other particles of comparable significance to itself. By this cooperative action it gains greater powers for itself and attains greater potentials of collaboration with the force. But it must still obey the immutable law to retain its own individual identity even as it extends itself. The new extended individuations, then, become, as a group, a new form, while further extension or action of the whole new form results in a transformation within the identity of the whole.

In phase four we see the form continue quantitatively as the basic security level, while extension is through the identity of the form extending self in qualitative transformation.

With the first self-sensitive or self-conscious act of a form, life is—not born—but able to show through the form as life. It is an act of experience rather than a reflex action. Directional motion becomes personal experience of individual identities. The experience promotes qualitative transformation within the identity of the form. After this first self-sensitive act, or experience, the factors of what we call life, or a living organism, become apparent within the form. We see one kind or another of self-reproduction, physical self-extension, growth, or self-transformation, and finally decay, entropy or physical death.

Qualitative transformation within one identity cannot be extended or transferred to another identity except through factors of inheritance. Knowledge is irreversible change after experience. It is not "book learning." These factors are somehow modified, refined, extended or sensitized by the weight of history added by a particular identity and are passed, along with the accumulated inherited weight of history, to the next inheritor. In phase four this inheritor is produced by self-reproduction. The qualitative changes within the identity (extensions of experience) pass into the progeny of that identity. By this factor such a form as man has been able to progress from fumbling subhuman forms to a more self-conscious state of being, though still fumbling. The qualitative transformation, which becomes an inherited tendency (DNA), is of a kind that advances an individual in growth or refinement of characteristics, thus serving as an extension in self-knowledge to the force of extension.

The extension of an individual in time is through retention as an individual identity, and it results in qualitative transformation within the individual. The more times the individual identity collaborates with the force in self-extension, the more sensitized and conscious the individual becomes, the greater the weight of history it carries within itself and the more modified its factors of inheritance become. Not all experience or activity of the identity results in modification of the inheritance factors. Only such experiences and actions as extend the identity in collaboration with the force do so, that is, only experiences that give the force of extension a new viewpoint or extension of consciousness of itself modify the inheritance factors. The modification within the identity's inheritance factors or genes are very slight modifications. They are only a tendency or greater sensitivity toward seeking the same kind of experience or exhibiting the same kind of action on the part of the reproduced progeny.

Only the experiences that have aided in extension are retained as inheritance factors. This is the evaluation of the form individual by the force. The useless actions or experiences are not passed on, this is the "forgiveness" of the individual's errors. The evaluation of the form individual is different than that of the form identity, for the form individual relates to continuing life or evolution of the form (the species) within the world's space and time. The form identity is evaluated concerning its continuation outside of space and time, what some may call Karma.

In phase four directional motion becomes personal experience, velocity becomes rate of growth (change), positive quotient becomes inheritance factors (natural modes of action), negative quotient becomes sensitivity or consciousness (how he may be acted upon), time becomes episodes of personal experience, and space becomes the area of observation or extent of action.

CHAPTER

10

Finding Ourselves

Are your body, days, manners, superb?
After death you shall be superb.
    Walt Whitman—*By Blue Ontario's Shore*

From the practical viewpoint, our own extension actually works out exactly conversely to what we might think we are doing when we act. We attempt to extend our objective, material, form or quantitative self, and we do so through actions and experiences. But the result is actually to draw more objective material into our being. We grow up, we grow fat, we grow old, we grow dead (death is a form of growth), while our identity, which we strive to maintain, is actually being extended in being qualified, in a kind of extension of thought, consciousness or character. We do have the physical extension into new individuation in our children, but this is a complete cutoff from our own identity, except for the inheritance factors. It does not retain our self-identity in the new individuation. As conscious beings, our offspring are extensions of God, not us.

The reason that our quantitative self is retained when we endeavor to extend it, and our identity is extended qualitatively or in consciousness, is that we are collaborating with the extension of the force, or God, who considers the spiritual to be the reality and the objective or material being to be a form of experience, somewhat less absolute reality than spirit. God's viewpoint and ours are ever at opposite ends of creation, looking at each other and demanding, "Why can't you see things my way, just once?" We must learn that God's viewpoint is the reality, and ours is the illusion.

Man's mind is the balance between body and spirit, with brain-mind, or sense perception, on one side and soul-mind, or will, on the other and reason-mind, or intellectual faculties, as the balance point. (See Figure 10-1.) This balancing is necessary for a spiritual reality to exist consciously in an objective material being within space and time. There must be a balancing factor, a go-between, if there is to be cooperation or collaboration.

brain-mind (sense-perception)	reason-mind (intellectual faculties)	soul-mind (will)

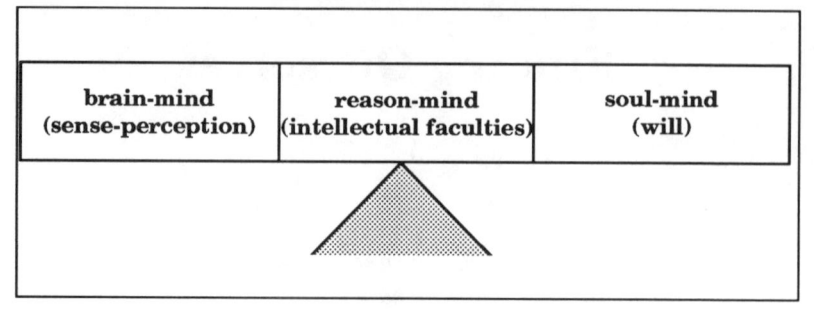

Figure 10-1
The Balance of Man's Mind

Man is one-fourth pure spirit, which is the viewpoint of the force acting through the individual. Man is one-fourth qualified spirit, which is his soul or individuated spirit in space and time. He is one-fourth form being, which includes all of his inherited form self and contains a weight of history since the beginning of extension. And he is one-fourth qualified form, which is his individual identity, qualified by personal experiences within the world of space and time. The balance point of it all is his reasoning or intellectual faculties. By soul-mind, or will, man recognizes his vital desires, his need for extension. (See Figure 10-2.)

By sense perception, or brain-mind, he weighs his environment, his opportunities, in space and time. By reason-mind he correlates his vital desires or soul-mind to his environment, thus choosing from the latter the specific means by which he may be able to achieve his vital desires.

Man lives in four dimensions of being concurrently, in a kind of lateral time scheme, though he may not be necessarily aware of all four time elements. It is the tension of equilibrium of these four dimensions of being (held within the four elements of time) that makes the individual sensitive to, and conscious of, stimuli proper to each dimension.

FINDING OURSELVES 75

```
          qualified  |  pure
          form       |  spirit
          -----------+-----------
          form       |  qualified
          being      |  spirit
```

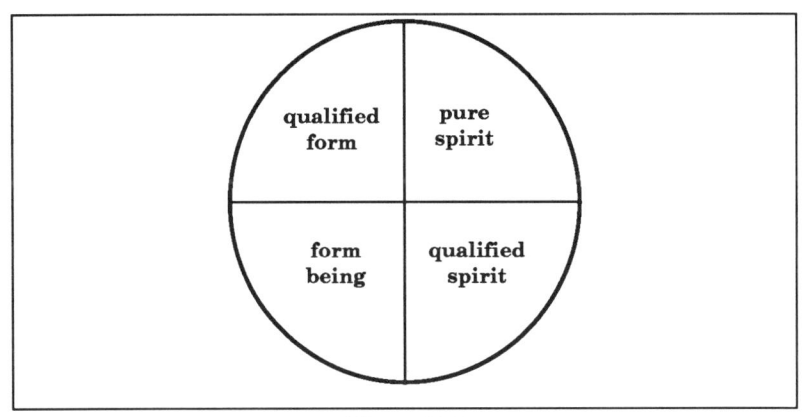

Figure 10-2
Composition of Man

Mind is the organ of symbolism. It functions as intellect. Intellect compares and conceives. Identity is the organ of evaluation. It functions as will. Will directs.

We can interpret the impulsions of the force to the individual as commands to "keep moving." They prod the individual consciousness to seek, do, know and act. These proddings arise in the individual consciousness as "vital desires," and they become fully conscious to the intellect as specific desires.

Man uses his soul-mind to recognize God's will. He uses his sense perceptions to discover himself in space and time, and to see what material he may utilize to fulfill his needs. He uses his reason or intellectual faculties to abstract the value of all his experience. These functions are, of course, separate functions of his one mind rather than several different minds, but the functions are so separate and unique that we emphasize that fact by speaking of separate "minds." Man also must have free will, exercised by his soul-mind, to choose between environmental values.

Man, therefore, is born with four natural freedoms or rights, which no one has the right to restrict in another human being as long *as they are sought in the proper order.* (See Figure 10-3.) The first freedom is the right and freedom to try to discover God's will and to carry out the rest of his freedoms in response to that will. This right is, by some means, the freedom of communion. The second freedom is the freedom to think, to reason for himself and to evaluate according to his needs and circumstances as long as his evaluations recognize God's will on the subject. The third freedom is

```
┌─────────────────────────────────────────────┐
│   ╭──────────────────────────╮              │
│  ( The Freedom of Communion   )             │
│   ╰──╮───────────────────────╯              │
│      ╭──────────────────────────╮           │
│     ( The Freedom of Thought     )          │
│      ╰──╮───────────────────────╯           │
│         ╭──────────────────────────╮        │
│        ( The Freedom of Extension   )       │
│         ╰──╮───────────────────────╯        │
│            ╭──────────────────────────╮     │
│           ( The Freedom of Evaluation  )    │
│            ╰──────────────────────────╯     │
└─────────────────────────────────────────────┘
```

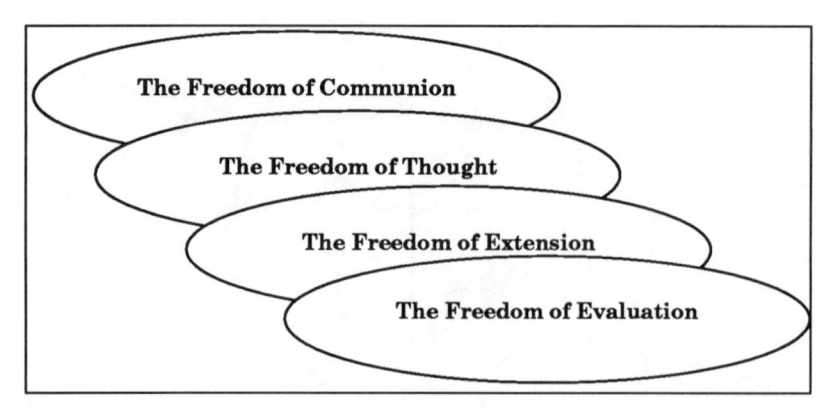

Figure 10-3
The Four Natural Freedoms

his right to experience, to extend himself in his own mode of action, as long as it is not done against God's will or against reasonable world evaluations. The fourth freedom is his right to suffer profit or loss for his own actions, to be evaluated *only* according to his own merits or demerits. This last is the freedom which allows each of us to go to hell in his own boat.

Theoretically these freedoms would mean freedom from limitation of bad inheritances, freedom from distortions of false precepts and teachings and freedom from useless or confining conventions and customs. Such ideal freedoms are impossible, but an individual must struggle to evaluate such factors and free himself as much as he can from their effects. We shall extend this topic in Chapter 13.

The primal force as free spirit is that which existed prior to any material existence and outside any physical limitations, but this does not mean *only* long ago and far away. It equally means here and now. Infinity is here, Eternity is now, just as much as they are any other time and place. Spirit is ever enduring, ever present, limitless, boundless, complete, whole, immediate and exigent: the forever now and the everywhere here.

Spirit is the manifestation of inherent power, the power to be, know or do according to the inherent capacities or capabilities of being, knowing or doing. Your inheritance determines your portion of power, your particular way or manner of knowing and your specific modes of doing.

Spirit is inherent in all matter or material existence, and is:
- a thing's inherent power to be, live, grow, develop and exist.

- a thing's inherent power to know, be sensitive to vibrations, to receive stimuli or to be acted upon.
- a thing's inherent power to do, act, perform, behave or react to stimuli or vibrations.

Matter is spirit with a history of being, knowing and doing. It is to be treated with respect. It is another aspect of spirit, a residue of the force as a historical event of the past that is yet part of the present, thus foiling "time" by coexistence of past and present. This coexistence plus the immutable law indicates the potential future. Thus the coexistence of past and present, the immutable law and the conceptual self-relations indicate that the future is also conceptually coexistent with past and present, though not materialized.

The purpose of a thing is to be, know or take one step further in any direction than anything has before. Extension is progression of spirit.

Inheritance indicates both capacity and limitation. We limit ourselves unnecessarily with our education, belief, traditions and emotions. An open mind, unprejudiced and unbiased; dares to push our capabilities to their outer limits, and to stimulate the imagination to develop new methods. New directions of action are essential to developing and using our inheritance to its fullest potential.

Dignity of spirit for ourselves, and honorable and humane treatment for all others should be our only self-imposed limitation and the criteria by which we forejudge and self-judge our own behavior.

God as Living Spirit is in constant and perfect "touch" with us at all times. We have only to "answer the telephone," so to speak.

Communion is our personal fourth dimension of being. However, it is only on the rarest of occasions that we are in any way conscious of that communion. While only man, insofar as we are aware, has conscious communion, everything in nature has communion of a kind. When man's individual spiritual consciousness and the Conscious Spirit, as it extends itself in self-experience within man, come into exact focus and become congruent, a new extension of God's consciousness through man is possible. The individual will have new revelations, intuitions or experiential knowledge of God's reality and extension.

Man is not just body-mind, body-soul, mind-soul or any of the dualistic interpretations. He is more. He is body, mind, soul and spiritual reality.

We must distinguish between form-man and racial-man. Form-man contains the weight of history of all that led up to the emergence of the present human type. The identifying factor of the true human was his realization of sense perceptions as something that he could react to through his own practical common sense choice of action. He could come in out of the rain. He became self-conscious. This realization gradually led to his full recognition of his own identity, which was coincident with God recognizing or evaluating him as spiritually conscious and responsible.

Racial-man has developed necessarily along a definite line of progression, because of the nature of the force, the nature of the material world of time and space and the inherent nature of the form-man. It is the line or direction or depth of development that is inescapable. The exact events were those that did happen out of various possibilities that might have happened, although the possible variants were not too many. The preordination of man was the result of existing circumstances. Events were in no way predetermined, but were narrowly circumscribed as to potential, and definitely set by the past as to direction. Because of the weight of history of the form-man, the history of the evolution of the racial-man had to develop in certain directions, at certain rates of attainment, and with certain modifications in the racial inheritance, which were passed on to all succeeding progeny. An individual born today lives through or recapitulates in his own development the entire history of the form, not in each tedious essay into extension, of course, but in its broad scope of actual attainment. He lives through the form-man history in his own development from his moment of conception to his actual birth, and through the racial-man history from his birth to his adulthood. After the age of 18 or so, the individual then concentrates on modification of his self-identified being.

We can expect that the pattern of development of each individual human being would follow the form history and the racial history of man, and so it does, and it further extends itself into its own spiritual development. These ideas will be carried out at length in the Chapters 11 and 12.

We have defined true knowledge as the change that occurs in our being when some experience passes through it so completely as to wreak an irreversible change. It is the individual self as quantitative being that experiences and absorbs the experience. It is the identity as qualitative being that evaluates the experience and extends it as conscious knowledge.

The highest attainment of man is experiential knowledge of Living Spirit, an experience that passes through one so intensely, violently and irresistibly that it may be a truly painful or terrifying experience. The only means to alleviate the pain or terror is by knowledge of the value of one's destiny. Without such faith the experiential knowledge can be agony beyond endurance. In experiential knowledge there is nothing serene or anemic. It is rather a psychodynamic thrust into the need for an action or an expression of the knowledge. Of such agonies are born ecstasies of revelations, mystic experiences and truly great art works.

The agony derives from the fact that at such a moment the individual longs to see that which is unseeable, to know that which is unknowable and to attain that which is unattainable, at least within the life of this world. Goaded by the violence of his desires, he may try by modes of violence to know, see and attain, but never with success.

We must emphasize that this experiential knowledge of God is not some secret that God whispers in our ear; it is God seeing or knowing Himself as existent in some phase of our personal experience. We recall that the purpose of God is to extend self, not to create things. Creations are incidental, though necessary. God's evaluation of the extended thing is after the fact of extension, but is evaluation expressed by the fact of extending Himself through this extended thing.

Left to God alone, extension would occur so fast that we could never catch up to even talk about it. But since the door to extension is opened through the action of individuated things, the individual slows up the process by his own necessity to be impelled to action, to choose the action from evaluated possibilities, and to act. Since it is the individual who lives in the world environment of space and time, it is the individual who must have free will to choose the elements from that environment that further his own extension, according to his personal inheritance and history.

Conscious Spirit exists concurrently to, but is not limited by, that space-time element. The responsibility of specific choice rests entirely upon the individual, and on his choice he will be judged. But God has not abandoned the individual. The more fervor with which one endeavors to solve a problem of his own extension, the more help he will receive. The more conscious or knowing one is of the facts and processes of extension, the more clear, apparent or obvious is the help received.

CHAPTER

11

DEVELOPMENT OF THE INDIVIDUAL IDENTITY

"Only the good is universal"
　　　　　　Walt Whitman—*Song of the Universal*

　　We have said that "identity" indicates the idea we have of ourselves existing, the recognition that we do exist and are individual. This recognition is what preserves the identity intact and does not permit it to be destroyed or dispersed. Once we formulate our idea of identity, we strive to maintain it. We do not necessarily have any particular idea about our self—the idea is only the recognition that we each exist as an individual of a certain kind of nature. It is our "time" being, not temporal of this world only, but our being relative to eternity. It is qualitative being. It evaluates our experience and extends it as conscious knowledge.

　　The idea of self existing as an individual is not born in us in our quantitative form being. It comes to us as a child at about the age of six or seven. This emergence of individual identity can be as great a shock to the child as the bursting of the embryonic sac. Like a light bursting, the child suddenly sees and thinks, "I am me" or "I am a person."

　　However he may articulate the intuition of identity that hits him about that age, he feels and knows something much more involved than his bald statement of existence. What he truly recognizes as a feeling, perhaps not articulately or even too consciously, is that he exists as a separate self in an identity separated from all other identities. What hits him with sudden astonishment is the fact that his individuality, his dissociation from the "whole" of something. It is not simply, "I am," but "I am I," or "I am John" or perhaps, "I am existing as John." He absolutely experiences the fact of knowing at that moment that he is John and not Bill and that John and Bill can each start off on the same road but go independently in different directions if they so choose. He recognizes his power of choice of action.

It is the moment of realization of absolute freedom of the self will, the free will, the dissociated identity will. This intuition comes to every human individual at about the same age, but to some it comes more consciously, and they may articulate a recognition of it. To others it is a fleeting feeling about themselves that they do not grasp or understand. But after this high moment of self recognition, their entire viewpoint of the world around them and the self within them is forever changed. They have been liberated into the life of the world, set free in space and time to thereafter develop the identities they have just discovered that they possess. The objective being has come into conscious experience or realization of its self as subjective being. But it has not created that subjective self.

At this point our story differs with Jean Paul Sartre, who believed that we create our subjective identity. We maintain that we recognize it but do not create it. If existentialism were true, the individual would have had to create the forces that brought the recognition of his identity to his consciousness. Of course the individual does not create those forces, nor their directives, nor the consciousness to which they arose. After recognizing his identity, the individual thereafter develops his subjective or qualitative self in the perfect freedom of his own choice. He even may choose not to develop it. We cannot agree that he creates that subjective self after a primal period of objective existence, any more than he created his objective existence. He merely comes into certain conceptual self-relations and thereafter more consciously develops his subjective being.

His subjective being is his qualitative self, and the quality that defines it is self-consciousness. He does not create his self-consciousness, but he develops it by adding to it in the future evaluations he makes of his experiences. He grows in self knowledge.

Sartre told us "We will to exist at the same time as we fashion our image." God may do so; we as individuals do not. Even God had to will to exist according to one definite image, in order to exist at all. He was immutable law but could not transcend the law of His own being, His Supra-nature, which is what Sartre would seem to claim man can do. Man cannot create the laws of his own existence, or he would have had to will to recognize his identity before he recognized it, and that he certainly could not do. Identity recognition is something that happens to him, because he is an extension of supra-consciousness, dissociated into individual consciousness (even as it continues in supra-consciousness). God's self, as God, does not extend; His consciousness of being does, and this extension of consciousness describes the potential of quantitative and qualitative individuation and individuals.

We can have concepts of knowledge rather than concepts of reasoning, but we must then reduce the concept of knowledge to reason, that is, to logic and experience, to make it intelligible to the understanding. So the initial concept of identity, the knowledge of self identity, must be developed by reason, judgment and discernment. This development does not create identity; it extends it in terms of life within this world's space and time.

"Consciousness" is mind knowing; it is not sense perception only. It is mind in action plus feelings. Feelings are the result of indecision or certainty in choice of actions. Emotions are the result of frustration or satisfaction of action. We distinguish between feelings and emotions.

The concept of self identity as a concept of knowledge indicates that the individual knows himself as an individual being who can direct his own actions. It is coming into conscious realization, not only that he exists as a separate individual, but that he may act solely upon his own directives. He may choose to go home to supper or go to the creek. Previously, our six-year-old child may have wandered off more or less absent-mindedly to the creek. Now he knows his power of choice. Since he equally knows the sting of a willow switch and the taste of fried potatoes, he will, if he is a reasonable child, probably choose to go home to supper. In other words he now reasons, applying logic and memory of past experience. Hereafter he will evaluate his possibilities and consciously choose. Ask a child of four or five, "Who are you?" and he will stare at you blankly. He does not know he is a subjective identity. Ask him, "What is your name and he will tell you. His name is an objective fact that he knows.

There is a further realization of identity at a little later age. At about twelve to fourteen the child comes, just as suddenly, into a realization of his identity as a spiritual identity. The idea smites him unexpectedly that he may also think and act from a viewpoint like that of the force. Of course he does not use these terms. Perhaps he begins to think of "the good of mankind" or some such viewpoint. The expression of this new intuition of spiritual identity, consciously acknowledged or not, and no matter how expressed, is a "declaration of faith."

In some way this new intuition is a recognition that God actually exists and that one is in God. Such a declaration establishes the identity of the individual spirit, the individual soul, which thereafter may be developed according to the pattern and mode of development that is natural to the soul's estate. We do not create our identities, à la Sartre, nor our soul, à la Alfred North Whitehead, but we recognize and develop them according to the pattern of development natural to them and through specific modes of attainment consciously chosen by the individual according to his personal evaluations and abilities.

Sartre and Whitehead both assume that the specific modes of attainment by which the pattern is developed is the ultimate reality, rather than an objective manifestation of a much more basic, primal reality. It is a fact that it is necessary for each form to translate the directives of the force of extension into terms relative to its own nature and for each individual of the form to retranslate the terms into specific terms relative to his understanding. This is the fact that allows Whitehead and Sartre to believe that the individual creates its own identity and its own soul.

Sartre says: "Man is no other than a series of undertakings, he is the sum, the organization, the set of relations that constitute those undertakings." And Whitehead says, "The soul is nothing else other than the succession of many occasions of experience, extending from birth to the present moment."

What holds this series of undertakings or successions of occasions of experience together? Why do they cohere within one individual and do not fall apart as so many isolated facts of living? Why does the development of identity and soul follow the same pattern in all human beings? Why is it that there is no development if the pattern is not followed? If each individual created his own pattern of development, there would be small similarity and never exact coherence to one pattern. (We shall outline presently what the pattern is.) What factor causes any development whatsoever? What factor energizes it? Why do feelings or emotions arise at one point or another?

Whitehead seems to have believed that the fact of succession, each occasion merging into the adjacent, is the glue that sticks all the acts of experience together. Does this glue add significance, or are the successions still but a string of interrelated occasions? Sartre tells us "There is no reality save action." But, for there to be action of any kind, there must also be something that acts as an agent of action even though that agent is intangible and non-material, and there must be, if not actual direction and specific intent, then at least some directive of action if it is going to result in anything other than blind chance action. And the action must be of some particular kind.

Are the agent, directives, and kind of action less real than the action itself? Has the result no reality? How can there be millions of repetitions of one particular kind of action and direction of development, as happen to individual identities, if the action is the *only* reality? For any organization to occur there must be principles of some kind that allow that organization to be and to be endlessly repeated. Each individual cannot create these principles from nothingness for himself. To blame it all on "human nature" only pushes the question back one more episode in extension. Do we each create our own human nature afresh? Or do we merely recapitulate the past of the form by necessity?

The pattern of development of the individual identity and the soul is established by
 • the nature of the force of extension
 • the nature of man as form, and
 • the nature of the soul.

The development is modified and materialized by the particular capacities, interests and limitations of each individual's inheritance and by his environment, and his particular place of being in space and time. These factors preordain his actions within certain areas of possibilities, a preordination not too finely drawn, but still definitely restricted by a limitation of possibilities. From the individual viewpoint, man is "ordained" by his inheritance of certain traits and capabilities from his particular family ancestors. He is further formed by his environment, which includes his education and experiences.

But space, time, ancestry and human nature have been derived by preceding modes of extension of the force itself, so we must go back to the ultimate source, the nature of the force itself, to find the true preordination of any individuated thing. In each *form* the directives of the force, to extend self and to retain identity, must be *translated* into terms understandable to the immediate state of the form. These directives, translated, are the glue that hold Whitehead's "occasions of experience" and Sartre's "series of undertakings" together.

We must remember that the purpose of the force is to extend self (to become), not to create something. For this reason we have not called it the force of creation. Its purpose is to extend self in such a manner that the identity not be lost, and the only way in which this can be done is through extension into dissociations of self, new individuation. The creation is a kind of by-product, and is not at all a thing aimed at, or a final ideal end. In the *extension* is the attainment.

We define a thing in its own nature (not by subjective, individuated viewpoint) by observing how it serves as a vehicle of extension to the force in action. To find the definition of a natural object or thing, we ask:
- Where is this thing found in its natural habitat?
- In what kind of action is it habitually engaged?
- What are the consistent results of its action?

We could define man by this formula:
- Where is man found in his natural habitat? Roaming over the earth and above and within the earth.
- In what kind of action is he habitually engaged? In adapting everything he encounters to his own use through experience.
- With what consistent results? That he reaches a better understanding of the interrelations of himself to the universe, so that he evaluates his experience and extends it as conscious knowledge.

Man is free. But this is not absolute freedom, it is only freedom to be man. Like all other existences, man must exist according to certain limitations and capacities that outline man-ness, the identity of the form. And he must endeavor to extend himself as an individual, as man in humanity and as a spiritual reality. That is the immutable law of his being. Man does not create his man-ness, nor his necessity to extend, and this nature and this necessity are the forces that direct his every action, no matter how freely he chooses a specific action. He is even free to choose not to exist like a man—he can vegetate like a cabbage to some extent, but such choices destroy his man-ness and his being.

The general purpose of man is the same as for all created or extended things—to collaborate in the self-extension of the living force. But specifically and from man's own viewpoint in space and time, his reason for being, his purpose, is to extend the consciousness of God. It is not to extend new ideas about God in man's consciousness, but to extend God's consciousness of Himself in individuated identities and experiences. Figure 11-1 shows man's patterns of recognition and response to other existences.

> **Stimuli:** vibrations emanating from other existence. We receive stimuli as sound, color, vision, odor, etc.
> **Reception:** receptivity of vibrations from stimuli; the kind and degree received is dependent on the nature of recipient (inherent capacities and limitations)
> **Perception:** awareness, perception, acknowledgment on some plane of consciousness of vibrations received; the kind and degree is dependent on sensitivities of recipient (largely inherent)
> **Conception:** assimilation and evaluation of vibrations received; the kind and degree is dependent on the inherent and educated capacities and limitations of recipient
> **Re-transmission:** reissuance or retransmission of vibrations in some form; the kind and degree is dependent on the capabilities and talents of recipient (largely educated)
> **Senses:** taste, smell, hearing, touch, physical sight, mental perception, spiritual intuition

Figure 11-1
The Patterns of Recognition and Response to other Existences.

"Consciousness" indicates "mind in action." (See Figure 11-2.) Actually the human mind exists only when in action. There is not a storehouse of ideas or perceptions called mind; there are habit patterns of perception. The more frequently one of these patterns is used, the more quickly and easily it may repeat itself when some association sets in motion the reflex that calls the pattern forth. Thus we forget something that is not often used, such as a foreign language. The habit pattern of perception called forth by the association of a word symbol or a sound has been too long unused and has been superimposed or in some degree distorted by superceding patterns.

Individual mind exists only when it is in the action of abstracting principles and ideas from experiences or perceptions, according to habit patterns of perception. To come to a new evaluation of that perception is to extend consciousness. The mind is always present, acting and perceiving at such moments; it is wholly conscious of its own actions, that is, mind is wholly self-conscious of its own existence, activity and state of being at the moment. Individual mind comes to self-consciousness only after the fact of perception. Consciousness also includes feelings, sense perceptions, emotions and ideas. Consciousness then, as all inclusive at a given moment, includes past habit of perception recalled to mind as idea or state of mind, present sense perception as new idea, and the comparison between the two (or

Planes of consciousness		Levels of action
	physical sensation	instinctive action
	emotional reactions	trial and error
conscious)	mental perceptions	learned reaction
intelligent)	reasoning (concepts)	harmonized actions
intellectual)	creative thought	pre-planned action
will)	spiritual awareness	spiritual purpose
psyche/soul)	spiritual intuition	spiritual collaboration
spirit)	experiential knowledge of spiritual reality	spiritual union

Figure 11-2
Phases of Consciousness and Levels of Action

more) ideas. It includes evaluation, reasonings, feelings and emotions pertinent to the occasion. Feelings are pertinent to the condition of the *will* at a given moment and emotions are pertinent to the condition of action.

When we come to discussing *will*, we come to the *directives* of every human action that ever was, is or will be. Every human action attempts one of two things—to retain identity or to extend self. If it does both of these simultaneously, it collaborates with the extension of the force's self, and the result is a new individuation of some kind. (God collaborates in every conception.)

Will, as directive of action, must be retranslated anew for every individuated form, and indeed, it becomes further translated within each individual of that form. In the form of man, the *will*, or directives of the force, comes into the consciousness of the individual as a deep urge, compulsion or feeling that becomes articulated in the individual mind as a specific translation of a vital desire. It involves a need for a certain kind of action to solve the immediate problem or alleviate the pressure of the vital desire. The pattern in which these vital desires arise is the same for all men, and the action chosen by the free will of the individual is the specific mode of attainment.

We could outline this pattern in a number of ways, with many divisions, sections and sub-sections, but we choose to do it according to some understandings we have already reached for consistency's sake, and to avoid the necessity of defining jargon.

Wherever you go, you take God with you. Be holy.

CHAPTER

12

VITAL DESIRES

*"In Thy ensemble, whatever else withheld,
withhold not from us,
Belief in plan of Thee enclosed in time and space,
Health, peace, salvation universal."*
                    Walt Whitman—*Birds of Passage*

Figure 12-1 charts out the vital desires of man. We might extend section II of the chart into "Man and his Public World," involving all kinds of cultural, intellectual, aesthetic, social, political, economic, industrial and atomic age problems, but these are not actually basic to the nature of all men, they only refer entirely to man in a 20th century industrial society, cultural man only, therefore we shall not enter into this discussion at this time.

To attain these vital desires, in whatever specific form he is conscious of them, the individual extends himself, his quantitative objective being, his form being, his body in action, even as he retains his subjective identity. There is manifested a new individuation, a new qualification of his own being. He is a "changed person," thereafter activated from a new viewpoint in space and time. These instances of "extending his body in action" are equivalent to Whitehead's "occasions of experience" and Sartre's "series of undertakings." But the actions are not creation of identity and soul, only extensions or development thereof. Reality lies at a much greater depth than these which are but objective manifestations of an individual's response to "life" to the impulsions of the living force. We could study these actions, occasions of experience or series of undertakings forever and never come to the slightest knowledge of the nature of reality or God or life.

THE ALIEN BOOK OF TRUTH

	Instinct	Intellect	Intuition
	PAST	PRESENT	FUTURE
Vital Desires of:	I. the form MAN	II. Individuals and the World	III. Individuals and the Force of Extension
Individual Man as Identity	relief from biological needs, hunger, environmental pressures, disturbances	self-realization, experiences, knowledge growth	spiritual identification
Individual Identity Relative to Space	companionship, social instinct	communication	collaboration
Individual Identity Relative to Time	physical safety and well-being	significant accomplishment	to endure in identity

Figure 12-1
The Vital Desires of Man

The desires as given in the outline are the ones vital to bring the individual to adulthood. Thereafter his problems will be mostly those of his environment, not of self growth, though of course refinement of his character as it first comes to adult level will go on throughout life. It is also possible that an individual might not develop beyond one intermediate stage or another, and it is possible that a severe strain, illness or shock might make him retrogress in evaluation and action temporarily or permanently to one of the former levels of vital desire. He might return to one of his earlier viewpoints, although he will never be exactly as he had formerly been. The intervening changes will still be within himself, but not consciously so.

Before the child comes into the world, he is sensitive to at least part of the first of these vital desires. The child will leap and kick in his later stages of development as a human fetus does when he hears or feels the vibrations of a loud noise. Also, of course, he receives nourishment. Once in the world he very quickly reacts to the need for relief from hunger. He expresses this vital desire in his instinctive crying until he is fed. His social instinct, which at this stage is mostly a need for physical companionship and tender handling, will be expressed a little later by his crying for the presence of mother or her substitute to which he has become accustomed.

Gradually he learns other ways of expressing this instinct, as he begins to recognize the necessity of his physical safety and well-being. At first, however, his measures to protect himself may consist of nothing more than sleeping with his head under the covers to protect himself from anything lurking in the dark. Up to this time our little friend has had no real realization of his own identity as we discussed it a short time ago. But at the age of about six or seven he comes to this sudden awakening of his own sense of being, and he thereupon leaves the age of wholly instinctive behavior in which he had relived and recapitulated the history of form-man up to the dawn of man with reasoning power and intellect.

After the recognition of his own identity, the child develops it through conscious desires for specific experiences, knowledge and growth—those factors that bring him to a wider, deeper self-realization. Next he experiences the vital desire to communicate some of his acquired knowledge and to have others communicate with him. At about the age of 12 or a little later, nothing seems so important to him as to have his identity recognized by some significant accomplishment. This is the age when he cleaves to heroes and develops some worldly ambition. Thus he develops his identity in the present tense through his own experience and reasoning powers in the world in which he has discovered himself living.

At about the age of fourteen, he comes to an equally sudden realization that in some manner, God is, and that he is in God. This is the age of confirmation. He may turn against his former religious training and decide that he is, after all, an atheist or agnostic, which is but a negative form of belief. However he may express, or thwart the expression of this declaration of faith, it is the *only* door by which further extension of his spiritual self is possible, the development of his soul. Man *is* a soul. God does not have a soul—God is spirit.

We have said that *form* is the basic security level of the individuated or quantitative being. So revealed religions are the basic security level of qualitative being. For the first seven years or so of his life, the boy has depended on his parents or tutors for spiritual shelter. At seven, when he recognizes his own identity and his powers of choice, he becomes a reasoning individual. He comes to the age of first communion, but this is an age when revealed religion, or learned moral precepts, are necessary in order to provide a moral code that the child could not possibly expound for himself.

The age of 14 is the age of confirmation, or reaffirmation by denial, of revealed religion and adoption of some philosophical substitute by which he tries to puzzle out his own beliefs. Later his faith in God's existence extends into the vital desire for some communion, or for some collaboration on a man-to-man basis with God. According to his natural bent and the accidents that have happened to him, he may now try to reach communion through prayer, or he may simply question the meaning of the unisphere and his own being. Then he will begin to ask what "salvation" means, and "life beyond death." He wants to endure beyond death in any number of ways, to leave a family bearing his name in the world, to have accomplished some useful work for the good of humanity and, if at all possible, to be assured that he, as an identity, will exist in some manner beyond the death of this world. In another place we will go more fully into the relationship of man and revealed religions, but here we wish to return to the way in which an individual recognizes the vital desires of his pattern of human development and what he does in reaction to those desires.

These vital desires are the directives, or *will*, of the force in action as it extends through the individual intellect of the human form. They are constantly being vitalized by the primal-state impulsions of the force. The individual feels these vital desires as they have been shaped by human history, but he may not be able to recognize or understand them in their basic form. He automatically translates them and thinks that he feels them as a specific desire for some specific thing. He wants to eat an ice cream cone, read a new book, paint a picture or go to church. According to his viewpoint, his place in the pattern of development, he plans a certain specific action to attain his specific desire. The presence or absence of opportunities that lie at hand in his environment and the capabilities and habits or limitations that he has all help to narrow his potentials of action down to a few choices. Partial or complete inability to plan any action will call up definite feelings, while partial or complete frustration of the actions carried out will call up definite emotions.

As the individual develops through the pattern of human nature, each primal or vital desire once satisfied will enlarge his capabilities and instruments of action according to the one that brought the desire to fruition. But the action that solved one desire cannot be used exactly the same to satisfy the next—it can only be an instrument of help. The next succeeding desire will call for additional action and refinement of the old in order to resolve the problem. When this new vital desire is attained, all the preceding vital desire attainments have to be reattained from the viewpoint of the desire where the individual is now standing, the point at which he has now developed.

Thus, a newborn babe acquiring food is one thing, accomplished through the fine art of crying. A mature man acquiring food certainly requires mature action—spearing a fish or earning a good day's wages to buy groceries. The human individual can get stuck in arrested development at any stage of this pattern development. Because his inheritance of capacities is not strong or refined enough, or because he meets with environmental set-backs that discourage his further actions, the individual can deliberately refuse to develop. He can be inherently incapable of further development, or he can meet with some accident or illness that so weakens his will that he does not care to develop. He can will himself to death.

At the moment of confirmation of faith, the moment of the declaration of his soul, and his dependence upon the infinite and eternal force, the individual actually turns his viewpoint of the world around and away from the viewpoint of individuated being, and he begins to view the world from the viewpoint of the force itself. The more completely and consciously he is able to do this, the more fully he will understand God, nature, and man. Even though he little realizes that he has so reversed his viewpoints, he will suddenly come to think of things as "backwards." In his most profound thoughts he will suddenly see some truth as the exact reverse to something he had thought before. Sense impression facts will seem to be less important than intellectual or spiritual principles. Instead of pessimistically believing that the material world is hurtling itself to some fatal and inevitable doom, he will believe optimistically that his free will allows him to salvage the more valuable factors of existence and to pass them on to some useful and satisfying future.

When, at any stage of his development, an individual finds the complete and conscious satisfaction of any one of his vital desires, he will experience a moment of absolute joy, a moment of quietude and peace in which he will be pervaded by a sense of fulfillment, justice and marvel. Such moments may come more completely, fully and frequently to a child than to a man because the child "knows" better how to relax his anxieties and enjoy himself fully. He has not yet learned to question the joy or to disperse it by overmuch thinking. Such a moment is the force of extension, extending itself through the self of the individual as a result of the action. The action retained identity of the individual (and the force) even as it extended the self of the individual (and the force). The result, if not impeded by accident, is a new individuation of some kind, a new attribute of character, a new idea extension of consciousness, or a new viewpoint—a new launching pad for future flights of fancy. But such an idea will encompass absolute "Truth," and such a viewpoint will be one of reality.

The developing psyche may react in several ways to the opportunity that misfortune represents:

- It might overcome after much struggle and hardship and thereby gain strength, insight, and advancement;

- It might struggle and fail to overcome the difficulty in all outward aspects, but still will gain some insight, strength and knowledge, advancing in more subtle ways;
- It might evade the opportunity, thereby gaining nothing, losing self-tension and indefinitely delaying development until such time as another opportunity might present itself.

To struggle, to extend and to develop is the attainment. Struggle builds strength, sharpens awareness, strengthens self-encouragement which is self-faith, and by acceptance or rejection moves toward a more harmonious, better balanced pattern of being.

The outline of vital desires is an outline of an individual's development in body, mind and soul; it is not an outline of his human inheritance at birth. For this reason we have given the development of his intellect before we give his development as an identity with a spiritual inheritance

Intellect necessarily develops before there can be any recognition of one's spiritual reality. During his early years the child accepts the religious or spiritual teachings of his elders, more or less absolutely, and it is not until his reasoning powers and sense of logic are quite well developed that he begins to question what he has been taught, and to give genuine attention to whether or not he has a soul. If so, what can it be, where can it exist, where does it come from, what is his relationship as a body identity to it and all the other questions that quite naturally arise? This is the time of his reaffirmation, his confirmation, the period when he comes to absolutely know, not because he has been told, but because he experiences the intuitive knowledge of his own spiritual identity. The soul with which the child is born is the seed of spirituality only. For the first dozen or so years of his life, he must be taught by human precepts about his relationship to his own soul and to God. He can develop spiritually only after he comes to the self-realizations that he has something called a "soul" and that he is spiritual. First, reason and will must be clarified and strengthened by each individual for himself before he can become a collaborator in the affairs of the spirit. He does not create his soul, he recognizes and develops it.

In all creation, or extended existence, the potential of being of a thing is seen in its form prior to its existence. It is seen as a potential in the individuation from which it is extended. In animal life we see not conscious reasoning, but the potential of conscious reasoning and intellect, and in man this potential becomes fact. So in man we should be able to see the potential of further extension.

To extend the consciousness of God, is not man's potential—it is his man-function, relative to the Supranature. But the next individuated level of being, pure spiritual being, is seen as a potential in man, whatever we might define as spiritual.

The exact categories into which we break up the idea of individual development into an outline are not the important things. They are but labels by which we identify that something real is here. The vital factors are the fact of recognizing that such a development exists identically for all human beings, a recognition of the kind of actions imposed on individuals if they hope to develop according to the natural pattern, and the significance that the various facets of the pattern have for the individual.

When the individual comes into spiritual identity and realizes his spiritual being, it does not mean that this is the first recognition that God has of the individual existing. It means that the individual first really *knows* by some kind of experienced intuition that he is not only the "temple of God" as he has been taught, but that he exists in God. He discovers that he exists as one small viewpoint from which God surveys the unisphere in a particular way from a particular point in space and time. A little later comes the notion of collaboration with God. "If I exist in god and He in me," our individual thinks, "then surely there must be some mode of intercommunication and power of interaction between us."

If our individual seeks this collaboration by praying for understanding and guidance in certain matters, such as making evaluations of experience, and in making a choice of actions, he will receive it in some way relative to his imagination and bent of acceptance. One man will have a dream, one a vision. One will get a sudden intuitive answer to his problem. Each will receive in the way he can best accept and use, simply because that is the way his mind works. Of course he can reject it. He can say, "But that was only a dream, a hallucination or my subconscious releasing something." He does not ask what his subconscious might be. Some scientist has told him he has one, and he uses the thought as a crutch to bolster up his sagging understanding.

The individual who has come into his self-realization as a spiritual identity no longer evaluates for the sake of his own worldly existence. He gets outside of himself and evaluates and chooses for the sake of "the long way of humanity." How can the experience he has, the evaluations he reaches, help clear the way and relieve the agony for those who will come after his time of passing? He must assume this responsibility of reaching his evaluations and making his choices from this viewpoint if he is to continue to develop and to endure. His own salvation becomes incidental.

The formula by which each vital desire overtakes the individual consciousness is somewhat as follows: First, our individual feels a surge of restlessness. The vital desire, stimulated by the impulsions of the force of extension, is stirring about and creating an unhappy, restless feeling. Next, it comes into his consciousness in the form of a specific desire, and the individual decides that this desire may be satisfied by one specific thing or another. The individual freely chooses the specific thing and freely chooses by what course of action he will obtain gratification of that specific desire. If he cannot choose because of various conflicts within himself or his environment, he will vacillate between various feelings and the desire. He can become neurotic.

Once a course of action is chosen and the action ensues, it will be accompanied by various pertinent emotions until the gratification of that specific desire is attained. Once complete satisfaction is attained, there will be a refinement of former habits of action, a necessary readjustment of all preceding vital desires to bring them into relation with this newly established viewpoint. This readjustment is not necessarily done consciously, but unconsciously, by resolving the urges and feelings that nudge him into uneasiness. When all has been readjusted from the viewpoint of the latest vital desire, there will be a period of assimilation of the total value of that vital desire. There will be a new conscious evaluation of his existence as it now stands in the individual.

No sooner is this assimilation somewhat complete than a new vital desire will begin to stir, and the whole process will have to be repeated from a new emerging viewpoint. If the individual learns to distinguish between his truly vital desires and his specific ones, he will not be so frustrated, unhappy, worried or broken-hearted when a specific desire becomes completely unobtainable or is taken from him. He will realize that it was not so important after all, and that only the more basic primal, vital desire must be satisfied. This is to say, "Not my will but Thine be done," for the vital desires of human nature are, after all, but the modes that the force of extension utilizes in the human form to retain identity and extend self. That which collaborates with the force endures; that which does not may continue to exist for a time thereafter but it cannot extend its Self.

The vital desires that we have observed are those sign posts set up by the history of evolution of human nature, as evidence that the force has passed that way. They are the residue left by the weight of history within the form. They are the qualitative transformation within the quantitative translation form. They are the methods by which we ordain our own future. For each individual these steps, vitalized by the direct impulsions of the living force, are translated again into the consciousness of the individual as specific desires, that is, as specific modes of attaining that more primal vital desire. It is important to recall that we do not evaluate a newly attained vital desire from the viewpoint or evaluation of the preceding desire. Rather all preceding desires must be re-evaluated from the new viewpoint. If we do not do so, we do not progress, grow or develop. Succeeding vital desires then may be thrust into our attention by someone telling us that we should do so and so, or we must think this and that, but we will not really understand or know what they mean. We try to adopt someone else's attitude and find ourselves floundering out of our depths.

When there are so many equally valid viewpoints, it is no wonder that there is such a conflict of ideas possible concerning the nature of the unisphere and its inhabitants. Only one overall viewpoint, such as that of the force of extension itself, can resolve the conflicts.

An individual lives neither in a vacuum, an ideal paradise, nor a state of single blessedness, but in a world peopled by many other individuals. Each has the same nature, the same vital desires, and the same rights of existence and attainment that he himself enjoys. Thus the choice of a specific mode of action to bring gratification to any of the vital desires must rest, not only upon his evaluation of what he believes he would prefer and might get, but at least equally upon the necessity that he not interfere with another individual's equal rights. This principle is the basis of social justice. It necessitates a compromise between individual desire and the rights of humanity, and it involves moral self-discipline.

Moral self-discipline is the only way in which every individual can extend himself equitably while retaining his identity in the complete pattern of individual development. When this extension can be done more or less perfectly by all men, a new individuation is extended—the social world of all human relationship, humanity attained.

Humanity is the sphere of action in which man concerns himself within the life of this world of space and time. We have said that when an individual comes to realize that he has a spiritual identity, he no longer evaluates for the sake of his own worldly existence. He gets "outside of himself" and evaluates for the long way of humanity. He desires to collaborate with the extension of the force itself, not only in his own spiritual development as an individual, which is his extension in time, but also in the development of human progress, in humanity, which is his individual development extended in space. In so doing, his personal happiness and his individual salvation are *incidentally* attained.

The real revolution will be the revolution of human nature as it turns to look back upon its own becoming and learns to compromise with its individual desires for the sake of the long way of humanity.

However, the *identity*, *free will* and *freedom of choice* of the individual must not be paralyzed or destroyed by the rule of some totalitarian or disciplinary state. The individual identity must continue in the freedom of the individual, even as it extends the self of the individual in such actions as will benefit, or at least not harm, all man.

Thus the problem becomes political as well as social, but it does not mean all men must exist under one political government. Such political rule as exists cannot so discipline an individual's rights and freedoms that these are destroyed. In so doing, a state would eventually destroy itself as the Soviet Union has. The only possible disciplinary action is self-discipline, as it works in various modes of social democracies in which individuals vote for their own rules of discipline by their own free choice and with full knowledge of what they are doing. Love of man for mankind would be a strong enough policy to teach such a discipline, but at this moment it does not seem immediately liable to universal adoption. Probably the only way in which humanity could be quickly united would be by some threat or danger coming from outside all existing sociopolitical groups, such as would equally threaten the safety of all. The threat of common annihilation by atomic wars is a threat from within; it alone is probably not strong enough to quickly unite mankind in a common endeavor. An outer threat, such as an invasion of little green men from Mars, might make us unite in some kind of makeshift humanity, but it would not be a true "kingdom of God" on earth.

CHAPTER

13

EVALUATION AND MORAL FREEDOM

*The soul has that measureless pride
which revolts from every lesson but its own.*
                    Walt Whitman—*Song of Prudence*

If we try to follow every moment of the course of extension through its various phases and within the developing individual identity, we cannot do so. First, from our individual viewpoint, the various phases and steps are discontinuous and do not ease one into another. Second, from the comprehensive viewpoint of the force itself, the process is not a single straight-line progression, but a geometrical deepening, widening and lengthening of lines of progression that keep branching out into new lines of extension with every new individuation. The "cosmic equation" is the only viewpoint comprehensive enough to capture all facets of extension in a single expression, and even that is concurrently progressing. Extension extends—it is never a finished product. The actual individuations or creations are not the aimed-for factors, but incidentals, even to the equation. The equation even extends concurrently to the individuated extensions in space and time. It is by this fact that "God knows" everything that happens. He "evaluates" every extension, and at the same time the free will of the individuation has chosen the action and the extension.

We have tried to speak mainly of laws of existences and of that which has reality of existence so as to make two points. First, man's consciousness in no way "creates" that which has reality of being. Second, reality, in general, lies far beyond man's consciousness or anything he may think about it, and only rarely can man's consciousness touch the reality. If we started with a definition of man's consciousness and categories of qualitative terms to describe things, we would never see anything at all but the insides of our own heads. However, when we come to discussing terms of *evaluation* by either the force or the individual, we must then directly concern ourselves with the insides of our own heads, man's consciousness, and we must ask, "How can man know, perceive or evaluate any experience, and what does his evaluation signify?"

We have observed how man exists within this world in four dimensions of body, mind, soul and spirit. More exactly these dimensions can be stated as
- body and senses;
- intellect, or abstracting and reasoning faculties;
- spiritual consciousness, which is soul;
- spiritual reality.

These dimensions are extensions of the infinite and eternal force in dissociated individuations. The dissociation is a discontinuity only as seen from the individual viewpoint. From the force's viewpoint, they are continuous extensions of self, although discontinuous from each other as individuated selves. From God's viewpoint, we each exist as a part or extension of His own being. Therefore, each individual has some contact with the pre-space, pre-time sphere of influence, for this continues concurrently to extensions in space and time. We are each geometrically involved in this fourth dimension of being, but we can view this involvement adequately only by trying to do so from the viewpoint of the force, not from our individual viewpoint in space and time.

There are as many different ways to look at and analyze the problems of men as there are men to look at the problems. Here we are principally concerned with maintaining a consistent viewpoint, not because it is the only possible one, but because such consistency eliminates the necessity of constantly explaining "how we should look at the problem now." It alleviates the constant strain of redefining meanings, and redirecting attention. After many years of trial and error, we have devised this one viewpoint as the most inclusive we were able to find. We make no claim to absolute or ultimate truth, but we do claim that this is a very practical viewpoint by which to gain some understanding of ourselves and our selves' relationships to the world of existing things and of ideas and of God.

In the history of nature we do not see evolution pass from one stage to another by slow gradual easing into the succeeding. Rather it occurs by sudden complete mutations. In the racial history of man and in the development of the individual, the step from one stage to another is not observable in a continuous motion, but each stage is seen as a discontinuous and separate step because we observe only one half of the action—the activities of the quantitative self that acts. We do not observe the continuity of the spiritual reality, the inter-relations of the eternal force with the separated identity. We do not see the impulsions of the force at work within the individual identity, nor the evaluations of the force as action is extended. There is a geometric complexity to the reality, of which we can observe only the outer part, no matter how many microscopes, telescopes, scalpels or mathematical measurements we employ. A science that deals only in quantities, measurements and serial progressions gets but half the picture.

The hidden, subjective or "other half" of the individual thing we are viewing can be guessed or observed only if we surmise the way in which it serves as a value of extension to the force of extension itself. In man this value is an extension of the consciousness of the Supra-nature.

In other things of nature this value is not always easy to guess. We cannot say that the value of water to God was to quench the thirst of His creatures, for water appeared long before there were creatures to have thirst. If it were so, creatures would have been preordained, and the way of extension into creatures would have been determined. But it is not so. There was freedom of extension at every phase, in every step of the way of extension, and in everything that has extended. God did not create water for the sake of creatures he anticipated making at a later date. Creatures that needed water were able to appear because there was water. Had there been no water, other kinds of creatures might have appeared.

There is freedom of extension in all things, at all times. The only *value* anything has to God, or to the force, or Supranature, is the way in which He is able to extend through that thing. Creatures having vision were able to appear, to be extended, because there was light that made vision possible. They appeared because some creature was striving to extend his sense perception beyond his limitations, propelled to do so by receiving the impulsions of the force of extension, commanding the creature, "extend thyself!" They appeared because further extension of the force could only be done through a new kind of action on the part of some individuation. An inherited or repeated action is only a continued action not an extension of action.

The first "living" virus appeared when, propelled by the force, some action was extended by a molecular "form" extending itself through a new form of action into new relationships with other molecules within its immediate environment. This new relationship was evaluated by the force as a means of extending itself into a phase of "living" things.

We cannot always observe the way in which an individuation has been evaluated by the force, but we can to some extent observe the "hidden half" of man's reality of being by observing the way in which man, as a conscious being, serves to extend the force itself.

Although viewed "objectively" by his sense perceptions, man's consciousness of the world around him, outside of himself, is a subjective evaluation. It depends on how he conceives of himself making use of these outer things. He evaluates them in terms of his own use, or at most, in terms that some other man might conceivably use. Even scientific studies evaluate by using terms of man's sense perceptions, such as temperatures, velocities, degrees of hardness and measurements of energies. *All* of these terms are evaluations according to the subjective terms of human perception and use. Man can in no way act upon or even reach a complete concept of the reality of spirit.

The overall character of God's objectiveness, which we call "consciousness" is God's absolute experiential knowledge of Self. It extends in each new space-time extension, not, however, as something that God never knew before. Rather it is a space-time manifestation of a concept of being that has always existed in the nature of God, in Supra-nature, but had not up to this moment been manifested as a "real" thing in "space and time." It was a *potential* of being, waiting for the proper conjunction of circumstances of being to bring it to materialization. There was no blueprint hung in some spiritual realm, ready to be built into the thing, but because of the nature of the Supra-nature and its extensions, it was possible that such a thing would sometime appear.

It is the thing that is extended into material existence that is evaluated and matched up to its potential of being in God's consciousness as eternally held experiential knowledge of self. The quickest way to grasp the objective character of God's consciousness is to think of it as the cosmic equation from which all things are worked out in extension. We must not let this thought destroy the personal sense of God, but recall that God is also spirit as well as consciousness. He has being as well as power, and He is Living Force in that He also acts. These are three functions of one Supra-nature, deriving their power, being and nature from it. They are functions that portray that which is living, conscious or self-knowing.

Each individual thing is the practical demonstration in space and time of some elements that existed as potential of being, or concept of being, in the factors of the cosmic equation. But these elements were not defined in a specific formula of specific being until the formula was put together concurrently with the manifestation, or material demonstration, in space and time. The free will of an individual chooses which of several possible actions to perform, and only then can the exact formula be put together.

The exact formula was a possibility, but not an inevitability to occur at a specific place in a specific time by a specific identity. The formula is concretized by the action, not vice versa. The formula is not preordained to the moment; it is only possible at some moment. The formula was assembled choice by choice, step by step, during the material past. The formula of being of a thing exhibits its reality of being, while its physical manifestation is an apparency, or illusion, relative to human senses and intellectual faculties in space and time. By this fact, a living force works out the equation which is not a mechanical bit of spiritual mathematics, as would be true if the formula of being for each identified individual were preordained or predetermined.

Man is entirely too eager to discover himself predetermined and preordained, for then he would be relieved of all responsibility to develop and to behave himself. He would simply say of his bad behavior, "But I had to do that. I could not help myself. It was preordained that I should. Why should I be punished?" And he would sit on his fat pratt waiting for the glory and reward that had been preordained for him just because he was himself, and not for any merit he had earned. And so it is most difficult for him to admit that he is not preordained for anything at all, but he is free. His freedom indicates his responsibility to work out his own reward. He must extend himself in accord to the way of extension, God's will, or not to extend and to be so evaluated by not being recognized as a way of God's extension. One will extend beyond the death of this life precisely as one develops himself to serve the way of extension.

The formula of being that an individual puts together for himself as he chooses and puts into effect his various actions, is his spiritual identity. Its evaluation or recognition in God (the assembled formula) is the individual's spiritual reality of being.

The individual function is to let God see through the individual that certain things, actions or experiences are to be valued in the way of extension within this world.

We can say that man's consciousness functions upon four levels of knowledge:
- factual or practical knowledge;
- functional or theoretical knowledge, ideas about things;
- intuitive knowledge of underlying principles or relationships of being; and
- experiential knowledge of reality or God.

The unisphere in its own nature is neither good nor bad; it just is. We relate aspects of the world to ourselves and label these aspects good or bad, relative to our desired use or desired escape from them.

In our concepts of evaluation from the human viewpoint, we call a good thing whatever helps us attain one of our vital or specific desires relative to our "form" being. We call it a bad thing if it hinders or takes away. We call it true if it helps us attain or satisfy a vital or specific desire of our reasoning self. We call it false if it hinders or takes away. We call it a beautiful thing if it satisfies or attains a vital or specific desire relative to our spiritual realization. We call it ugly or perverse; if it hinders or takes away.

Such evaluations are man-made concepts relative to attainment of his desires within this world. Such evaluations of definite objects are relative to the time, place and person making them.

God, however, makes evaluations that are coextensive to the duration of man. We call such evaluations evil, error, moral good or righteousness. Through the Supra-nature, purely objective evaluations are made as a matter of extending or not extending through the new individuations.

The impulsions of the force for all men (not just oneself) implies:
- God is not law-giving, but extends immutable law.
- God is not loving, but extends divine love.
- God is not just, but extends absolute justice.(without specific individual object—therefore without caprice or partiality)

Sacrifice has no value except the limited sacrifices required by cooperation with men (responsibility) and collaboration with God (duty). As extensions of God's self, we have no right to sacrifice ourselves by destroying or submerging ourselves in other identities for any reason. For social justice, there must be an absolute balance of rights between all individuals, their institutions and relationships.

What is evaluated in man is not his intentions or his feelings, but his actions and experiences. It is not enough to think that you are good, you must act in a good manner, if it is only to articulate what good is. Otherwise the good has no real value.

What the force has extended is morally good and righteous if it extends itself.

What the force has extended is evil if it does not extend itself to the extent it is capable. What an individual has extended is ethically good if it extends itself (as a social organization). What an individual has extended has no reality of being and no life if it does not extend itself though it may be temporarily useful to the individual.

Since morals concern the practical manner of cooperating and getting along in the material world, the moral evaluation of an act does not lie in its intentions, however good, but in its practical results. Responsibility is placed squarely and completely on the individual who acts. He must choose prudently his course of action, and to do so, he must develop a sense of the long-range consequences. Moral freedom implies moral responsibility of each individual.

For a molecule the secret of a successful relationship is to tolerate and cooperate with other members in that relationship, not for the sake of the other members, but for the sake of the relationship. Only in the sphere of human love may we become conscious of this principle of relationship, transcend the principle, so to speak, and preserve the relationship for the sake of the other members involved.

The statements "The Kingdom of God is not upon this earth" and "The Kingdom is within you" seemingly contradict each other. The kingdom within are the evaluations of this earthly life relative to the viewpoint of the force acting. That it is not upon this earth indicates that these evaluations are not relative to individual existence in space and time. It is God's evaluation of spiritual reality individuated.

Such ideas as the kingdom of God is heaven, God is in heaven, God is within you, and your body is the temple of God indicate the continuing sphere of action as God forever exists concurrently to extensions of individual being in space and time. Concurrently to, but not of space and time. The individual must never get the notion that he is God, but only realize he serves as a vehicle of God's extension, both as an individual identity in space and time, and in the God identity that is not subject to individual consciousness, but is possible to be experienced as intuitive knowledge about reality and one's relation to God, and as communion of some kind with God.

In the "habit patterns of perception" of sense memory, patterns take shape from the evaluations we have made of an experience we have passed through. The evaluations made of an event that relates to a memory of experience of precisely the same kind is not a new evaluation, but one of degree, as good, better or best.

The more consciously we concentrate upon evaluating what happens to us as it happens, the more vividly we may call it up in memory.

To simultaneously know and evaluate an experience is to touch the reality of one's own being, for it is in such simultaneous experience-evaluation, or experiential knowledge, that man, as spiritual consciousness, and God, as conscious spirit, meet in mutual knowledge.

Man's consciousness of self-being extending in space-time has left an inheritance of cultural history. It is written in various places and times and in various ways, each separate way relative to, necessary to, and modified by, the specific time and place in which it appeared, that is, molded by its own inheritance or weight of history. Cultural history is how humanity as a whole, not only the individual, has developed through various stages of extension.

When the young adult at about age 18 who has developed his personal identity as far as possible finds himself ready to evaluate for the "sake of the long way of humanity," he discovers in his cultural environment many already conceived and established instruments and institutions by which he may extend himself as a member of humanity. These instruments are the beliefs, groupings, organizations or institutions established by the cultural history of mankind. From them our young man will pick and choose those that are evaluated as good, worthwhile or expedient to his particular circumstances. His evaluations will be, in one degree or another, conscious and dependent on his degrees of perception, reasoning and self-discipline. Thereafter the major portion of his life activities will be directed toward study, evaluation and self-experience in relation to these cultural ideas and institutions.

Such cultural concepts cover every area of man's thought—aesthetic, religious, scientific, philosophic, intellectual, political, social and economic. They include productive and industrial problems of the world as well as emergent problems of the nuclear or space age, which is extending so greatly the scope and value of man in space and time.

The individual identity, its power and being, must not be lost, destroyed or dispersed in any of these cultural concepts or institutions. The institutions must exist as instruments of further, more conscious self-extension of each individual and for all individuals as equitably as possible.

The individual is morally responsible to cooperate with the cultural institutions and social mores of his place and time, but the cultural establishments have an ethical responsibility, if not to actually further the extension of individual identities, then at least not to thwart, in any way, the proper extension of individual identities. Certainly, no cultural institution, whether social, political, religious or educational, has the ethical right to deny the integrity and value of any individual identity. Moral freedom of that individual must endure, and it can do so only with the ethical responsibility of all human groupings or cultural "forms."

Social consciousness must extend as social conscience. It is the conscience and strength of the institution to serve the individual, and it is the conscience and the strength of the individual to cooperate in the formation and maintenance of the practical institutions. For this cooperation to be properly done, each instituted body of men, each cultural institution, must serve only its own one phase of culture. An economic institution must be purely an economical function and not political. A social institution must be social and not industrial. Such purity of function is, of course, an ideal, but it should serve in the only way that an ideal has any meaning or any existence, as an indication of the direction and measure of extent of institutional action. "Render unto God that which is God's, and unto Caesar that which is Caesar's."

In the past, institutions have entered into areas of action outside of their own function only because certain human areas of welfare had not been touched by institutions proper to their nature. Someone had to do it. In the future, more precisely defined areas of function would seem to be advisable. We can make only cautious, general statements here for it is not within the scope of this presentation to enter into detailed discussions. We wish to present the subject of extension in the most stark outline possible, for only with a comprehensive grasp of the subject as a whole can the details be rightly evaluated or appreciated.

No people may live together in any degree of harmony if their sense of values are too diverse. Small differences may be overcome by sheer good manners, but manners alone are entirely too sheer. Before any establishment of "good relations" or functional peace, there must be some mutual acceptance of mutual evaluations. It is because of the lack of any mutual evaluations that the history of the many peoples of the world has been one of constant conflict and violent misunderstanding.

The effort must ever be toward mutually shared, or at least mutually understood, values. These values are moral, ethical and spiritual values, for it is only from these that a functional peace may be evolved, one that will then permit the attainment of the material values expedient to the times. This does not mean there has to be one arbitrary standard for all men on all occasions, but it does mean knowledge and tolerance of each other.

Manners, habits, dress and racial characteristics may be as different among men as night and day, but the values men live by must be mutually tolerable. Coexistence may be a healthier balancing factor than unanimity as far as practical working results within an imperfect world are concerned. Only gradually at least, event by event, struggle by struggle, can concurrence be perfectly established. It will not be soon.

CHAPTER

14

The In-Forming Spirit

*The potent, felt, interior command
stronger than words,
A message from the Heavens
whispering to me even in sleep...*
  Walt Whitman—*Prayer of Columbus*

There is yet one further step an individual may make in which the individual achieves a sense of union with absolute reality, a sense of the individuality or personal self being lost in the sense of oneness with the universe. It must be experienced to be truly known, and the experience is a whole thing, not easily broken down into separate words.

The in-forming spirit dwells within each of us in a realm that is reached by experiential knowledge, intuition and conjecture. Possibly most of what we say here is but a fumbling after truth, but the effort must be made, even tentatively, as an indication that there is something true there that can become known under proper circumstances. The actually acquired contact produces the most uncanny joy and peace.

We have not yet found the loom on which to weave our pattern of ideas in this phase, so we can offer only a shifting design of light and shade—like shadows of breeze-tossed leaves on a wall.

We have said life as we live it sometimes seems to be but a pale reflection of real life as it is being truly lived somewhere else in the unisphere. Perhaps "true life" is the state of our being, our actions, thoughts and feelings, as they are known to the in-dwelling spirit, while our individual consciousness of these events is the reflection of that Supra-consciousness.

We have said that the purpose of the force is not to create something, but to extend self, ever to become. We have also said that the dissociation of self into new individuations is the only way in which extension of self can be done by that which is already All-Being. The creation is a kind of by-product and not at all a thing aimed at or a final ideal end.

Thus from the viewpoint of the force itself a man's soul, his individuated spiritual portion, is not the final purpose of individual souls existing.

In order for extension of self into dissociated individual souls not to disperse the identity of the force in its phase of becoming, there must be the retention of individual souls within the subjective being of the force, and there must also be the continuation of the force in its phase of ever becoming. This continuation takes place within every extended individuation, not as part of the individuation's self, but as the ever-becoming of the force's self. We say, therefore, that man not only has a soul, witnessed by his own identity and will, but he also contains an area in which the force's self as spirit moves and has its being in its own phase of becoming. This area is not a part of man's consciousness or being, but is an area of man in which the force has movement and being, undivided from itself. It extends from everything that is, into everything else that is. All is one. This is the in-forming spirit.

The in-forming spirit fills this area of man's being with the direct impulsions of the force. It exists, not as a neat little room, one-fourth the area of man's being, filled with pulsating vapors, but as an interpenetrative part of every pre-substance particle of every cell of the living man.

Thus the body itself is truly the temple, but the materiality as body or form and the functions of the body itself mustn't be considered in any degree holy or to be worshipped. The body is to be respected, cherished and disciplined as a place of being of the in-forming spirit. Only the spirit is to be worshipped, and worshipped mainly in acts of gratitude and joy. It must not be worshipped as life, or limited life forces, but rather as Living Spirit. Here, conceptually, the impersonal law-giving force becomes the in-forming personal spirit. The individual man lives in constant touch with the source of his being, as it exists, not only within the particles of his own body, but as it exists in every particle of space around him, and in every particle of being in the unisphere. All is One.

The in-forming spirit is within us, but not of us. We must never get the notion that we, or any part of "us," is God. It is the self of God within us, not the self of the individual. The individual has his soul-identity self, existing in space and time, each individual self discontinuous from every other.

When it becomes evident to the individual that All is One, it becomes evident also that the quotation should not be, "There but for the grace of God go I," but rather, "There in the grace of God go I." Sympathy for humanity on the basis of this first statement becomes sentimental and probably insincere. On the basis of the second statement, it becomes empathy and commitment.

I stand at my window looking down the city street, and I am suddenly some Colossus astride his harbor with my back to the sea, looking down on a far stretching cluster of buildings of the city itself. I see into each roof top, watching the intimate comings and goings of people.

Or I am the dead pigeon, caught in the fork of a tree in the park. My feathers are wet and heavy upon me. My neck is limp, and my eyes closed. I am cold, so cold. My mind is empty in death.

Or I am the man with the aluminum crutches making my way along the broad walk beneath the statue. I feel the strain of the muscles along my lower back as I drag my unresponsive limb forward. There is a pull on my chest muscles and pain under my arms. And, oh, the weary tediousness my mind feels as it leaps ahead and ahead of my dragging feet.

Or I am Jesus, pinned on the cross. The pain of wounds in my hands, side and feet is nothing compared to the anguish from the rejection of my bountiful love. I am all things. I am with God and God is All.

These thoughts of course, are but a feeble reaching out for the attribute of oneness. They in no way approximate the actuality. They are thought exercises by which my mind's self lets go of its Self to prepare for the actual experience of being one .

The experience cannot be reached by desire or will, for it is beyond desire and will. One can put oneself in readiness by letting go of desire and will, by letting go of the conscious thought of self.

Here again we do not wish to intrude on the personal how, but only to suggest that such an experience is possible and that it can be reached through self-discipline, spiritual growth and study.

The individual soul self is identified in the consciousness. It is the individuated spiritual consciousness (or superconscious) of the individual. The in-forming spirit is in every particle of the individuated being. At the moment of realization of oneness, the entire body seems suddenly to be without weight or corporeality, somehow lifted or carried aside from the space it had just occupied. It is not the same sensation as partial dissociation, for in this, one has the feeling of the self watching or listening to the self from a little distance, the self being in two places at once.

In this union with the infinite and eternal spirit, the individual identity is not merged or lost, for it has always existed therein. Rather, the consciousness of the individual self is laid aside for a moment so that the forever-held contact with the All-Being may be consciously realized.

One of the most difficult problems the intellect can set for itself is to discover the reality of being amid the illusions. For nothing is altogether what it seems.

CHAPTER

15

Conclusion

*I know that the past was great
and I know that the future will be great
And I know that both curiously
conjoint in the present time.*
                    Walt Whitman—*With Antecedents*

This mind in action, this consciousness, impelled by the spirit (as impulsions), as all reality is, in man is called the psychic factor. It depends on his racial inheritance. The unique outline it subjectively assumes within the inherent capacities and limitations of each particular individual is objectively displayed as his personality and is subjectively held in what was once called his "soul" in old-fashioned terminology.

Modern psychologists too quickly branched away into purely objective studies of the material brain activities and left the recognition and study of this soul, this subjective reality, this psychic consciousness, the most vital study of all, to a few dedicated individuals scattered here and there. Any attempt to publicize the activity or its results too often met with derision and seldom with respect or even tolerance. Fortunately the scene is now changing. Once again one may speak of "soul" without ducking.

The answers of psychical research, parapsychology and psi are perhaps the only answers to the perils man has created for himself with his stupendous advances in materialistic sciences.

A force exists only when in action. It must manifest in order to be. Mind is a force. It exists in action.

Spirit is a potential to be, to know or to do. As potential, it always exists. It manifests as force. Spirit manifested is mind force.

Force in action is power:being, a composite of two forms of existence in one personalized nature.

Mind in action is spirit manifested as power:being composited as consciousness (a facet of nature).

Subjective mind is a real existence in itself, separate from the mechanics of the physical brain.

The objective brain recognizes and translates reception of stimuli from the environment.

Thoughts, ideas and concepts do not originate in the brain. The mind translates these receptions into symbols recognizable and usable to the individual experiencing them. We do not have "thoughts." Thoughts have us.

It is how we interpret what we receive, how we evaluate our experience, that expresses our own plane of being.

The old certainties have lost their hold upon our imaginations. The brave new world of nuclear destruction and space adventure is upon us here in the immediate now. Even the old questions call for a redefinition of terms before even tentative answers may be propounded.

Identity is the question of "Who are we?" Cause is the question of "Why do we do what we do?" Purpose is the question "Why are we here?" These are the big questions and the lost or never known answers.

Matter is the vehicle that holds and transmits experience. We are the experience of the past; we cannot escape it.

Before we can live effectively, we must define what we mean by living, and before we can be true to ourselves we must define what we mean by being true. Even more vitally, we must define ourselves.

If a man can know that something exists, he can also know what it is and why it exists, and what is his relationship to it, although his knowledge may be tentative and incomplete.

Any mystery is admissible of study; there should be no prohibition against questioning, analyzing or dissecting. As long as the existence is related to his existence, the study is proper and in order.

If we try means of forcing nature or other existence to reveal their secrets and hidden mysteries to us, we are being uncommonly foolish. All is revealed in that it stands transparent in its own nature; it cannot conceal itself. What we need to do then is to develop our own powers of seeing, hearing and knowing. Develop *ourselves* and we can read the hidden mysteries like an open book. We develop ourselves physically, mentally, psychically and spiritually. These are the four planes of receptivity open to us.

As a way of questioning:
A thing exists, or it does not exist,
If it does exist, what happens to it...
- with respect to itself?
- with respect to all other things?
- to all other things in respect to it?
- to all other things in respect to themselves because of it?

Our consciousness, molded by reason alone, must be our guiding star. There is no other. But we must remember too that consciousness has four facets: physical, intellectual, psychic and spiritual. Physical consciousness is sense perception. Intellectual consciousness identifies and integrates perceptions into ideas and symbols. Psychic consciousness is the subconscious, or racial consciousness. Spiritual consciousness is intuition, or experiential knowledge of reality

Emotions are part of human inheritance, but what arouses specific emotions are the results of one's thinking, consciousness and character.

If we have become soul-blind, it is not because our materiality ever carries a greater weight of history, for at the same time our psyche or soul has become ever more sensitive to the impulsions of the force. Rather, it is because we have lost sight of the meaning of what happens to us. Our specific desires have become our vital desires, and our values have become inhuman, or at best, dehumanized.

The only purpose of life is to live in accordance to our highest concepts. The only respectable goal is achievement—to go one step further in any direction than anyone has gone before. Achievement must be done in collaboration with the free spirit (not the experienced spirit, which is matter). Each of us is a unique viewpoint of spirit in space and time. To be true to "oneself," that is, to one's place in space and time, is all that is required.

Achievement—is a personal triumph of extension, the most exciting purpose one could ask in life, and each person to his own purpose, freely chooses experience as an expression and extension of his individuated identity.

The highest virtue you can practice is to hold your own life and achievement as a supreme value.

Men must be judged and treated for what they *are*, not for what they might have been. They made themselves, as they are, because that is all they were capable of. If this seems harsh judgment, consider someone who has become a worthy character in spite of reverses far greater than that which deformed another character.

Charity is to ask nothing for oneself that one is not willing for every man to also have, if he can get it for himself with equal honor.

To bankrupt self by giving one's wealth or self away in bits and pieces helps little and destroys an individual's own power. A wise man does not distribute or hoard his capital. He invests it and uses it to produce a steady flow of power that he can spend in good works.

To be dishonest in act, thought or belief, is to complicate life into confusion and to destroy one's capacity of straight action and true attainment.

Value indicates a choice of alternatives. Only a conscious existence has power of choosing (free will) for itself.

An instinct is the knowledge to do without thinking, choice, or even self-consciousness, something that is necessary for survival or life benefit.

Most of the acts we call living are simply acts of defying death. Hoarding a cellar full of potatoes is not living. Eating a potato is.

Dreams are perhaps subconscious evaluations, or evaluation by spirit. Some dreams are revelation of evaluations going on in the subconscious. Sleep is a time of evaluation of the day's reception.

We reach spiritual identity (I am) through psychic purpose (I will). By perfecting our psychological pattern, we perfect ourselves toward a better spiritual identity, and we have a "better" spiritual self.

The experiences and events through which we pass are the vehicles by which we consciously pass through the already completed, already laid-out, already finished tapestry of our event of being. We choose our own vehicles when we choose what we are going to do next. The final goal has already been determined by immutable law, by the formula of individuated being, and by our point of consciousness, i.e., our presently developed state. Who or what we are at a given moment is the sum total of our inherited past, our weight of history, the past of our individual lives and our analysis thereof, plus the circumstances, opportunities, and limitations of the moment.

The vehicle of event is simply the mechanical means by which our material body keeps up with the journey of the consciousness. The consciousness could reach the same goal much more easily, if it were not for the physical self it has to drag along. Consciousness is the built-in baby-sitter minding a rather idiot child as it tries to pick its way through a physical existence. Sooner or later the physical will falter and be left behind, too worn out, too crippled, too diseased, to keep up with the consciousness that will be freed for a different mode of travel.

To be virtuous for virtue's sake, rather than for hope of reward, is surely one of the highest attainments. Yet there is one higher in the field of virtue—to do good, to be good because one is incapable of any other kind of action—this is the supreme. This is ecstasy.

The immutable law encompasses many factors; its immutability is but one. It also is absolute justice, wisdom and love. These attributes are the humanized terms of the cosmic equation.

The workings of the law are more real than we are ourselves, as separated individuations of material, physical existence. Our task in life is to become more real. It may be that the mental state one has established or the psychic state one lives in subjectively will become the objective state of our next life. The subjective becomes the objective, and we thus create our own "heaven" or "hell" precisely as we now are or think.

CHAPTER

16

Afterword

*The Earth remains jagged and broken
only to him or her who remains jagged or broken.*
     Walt Whitman—*A Song of the Rolling Earth*

"This sounds interesting, but I am not sure that I really understand it."

So many truly intelligent people have said this in reading the foregoing pages that I have to admit that the fault is not in their intelligence, but in my presentation. Therefore I must clarify.

Had I started this study at my present age of 78 instead of 15, would I have written my three-factored formula differently? (The first thoughts were, of course, greatly expanded and restated during the ensuing years.) After asking myself the foregoing question recently, I spent a number of days in solemn consideration, and the answer is no. The basic formula is stated as exactly, explicitly and concisely as I can conceive. Perhaps the problem is that it is too simple. What is so basic must be so simple that it may apply to every object of real being in existence.

The simplicity of the formula is its undoing. My intelligent and cherished friends are expecting some convoluted, mysterious and esoteric, if not outright miraculous, formula. To be met with something so easy and straightforward throws their minds off the track.

But the formula should be clarified by example. We can use any natural phenomenon—atoms, people, stars or planets, for example. Let us take the factors of the formula of extension one at a time.

- **Factor One:** The self is extended.
  The particular natural body we are observing, whatever its nature, must extend itself in *motion*, *activity* or *experience*. The particular kind of extension is dependent on the particular kind of body.

- **Factor Two:** The identity is retained.
  The particular motion, activity or experience of that body must not change that body in such a way that its significance to nature is lost. An atom of Hydrogen remains an atom of Hydrogen regardless of its greater experience.

- **Factor Three:** A new individuation is released from the body that brought it into being, and thereafter it extends itself.
  This concept reaches beyond the recognition that a person has a child, for example, or that an oak tree has acorns. Two atoms of Hydrogen and one atom of Oxygen extend themselves into a combination that forms water. Water in turn can combine with other natural products, such as elements within the human body, although the character of the water is not lost. The identity of the Hydrogen and Oxygen atoms are not lost. The natural properties of water are not the same as the natural properties of its constituents. It is an individuation, just as Hydrogen and Oxygen are individuations. These atoms, in turn, are extended from the activities, motions and experiences of still more basic identities such as electrons, which in turn have extended from still more basic particles of matter that physicists are now naming for us.

Instead of using atoms, as an example, let us apply the formula to human beings, starting with the first factor, the extension of self. An atom must follow certain laws of its being; to act differently would destroy itself. An animal may act from learned habit or from the résumé of habit born into it, which we call instinct. To be human is to add a quality or characteristic that is lacking in other bodies. That missing quality is the ability to abstract values from experience and to retain them in mind for further use. A person may abstract and apply. He also may produce children, which, of course, completes the formula, but he also may fulfill the three factors without contributing to overpopulation of the planet.

Let us picture a still-young man nearing 40 who has a secure, well paying job, excellent health, a devoted wife, two young sons, a front pew in church, two cars, a boat, season tickets to the symphony and a complimentary pass to all local football games. He has everything that a nearly 21st-Century man of his circumstances could ask for, and he appreciates his blessings.

"Why, then," he asks himself, "am I so restless? Why am I at loose ends? Why do I feel so apathetic?"

His restlessness grows. He snaps at the kids, growls at his wife, pushes the aged dog out to sleep in the garage and hates himself for doing all of it. He needs to extend himself.

Then he sees a TV segment on bony, shrunken children starving to death in Somalia. The pictures haunt him as he eats his evening meal. He reads and hears talk about homeless people barely existing in the United States. He begins to notice wandering scarecrows in his own town. He sees ragamuffins digging through dumpsters and garbage cans for a bite to eat. He finds a young couple and their baby half-sheltered from the rain in an open shed in an alley.

He fulfills the first factor by extending himself in activity, learning all he can about local aid available to the homeless. He finds where the holes are in the safety net. He rounds up friends, businesses and social organizations and begins to knit together an informal, cooperative group to find emergency shelter and long-term solutions for the homeless of his town. His self-concept changes, but he *retains his identity,* thus fulfilling the second factor.

The activity of the new group snowballs. There are splinter groups organized, loosely but securely, in neighboring towns. He fulfills the third factor in that a new individuation, the aid group, has evolved from his extension of himself. The formula has been fulfilled. The young man finds everything in his own life has shifted to a new dimension. He has changed and evolved within himself.

Certainly the group must not be so tightly knit that the individual loses his identity and becomes one cell in an organization so tight that its members no longer dare to think or act within their own originality. Ants and bees have wonderfully evolved complex social structures, but they cannot evolve or even exist outside of their hive.

I hope that this little example reveals how simple the formula really is and how it is, at the same time, so basic that it undertakes the schema of the unisphere.

Special Acknowledgments

It would be impossible to mention all the persons who have been helpful to me in many kind and generous ways. To the following goes my deepest gratitude:

- Dr. Brian L. Crissey: for devising the diagrams for this book from my rough sketches.
- Pamela Meyer and her editorial assistants: for putting band-aids on my mangled manuscript.
- Hartmut Jäger of Kallaroo, Australia: for his illustrations in the front and for the God Dreams poem.
- Dr. James W. Deardorff: for his advice and critique, which resulted in advantageous changes.
- Dr. R. Leo and Marilyn Sprinkle: for friendship and hospitality when personal encouragement was much needed.
- Dr. Berthold E. Schwarz: for his ever-sustaining friendship.
- Dottie Burrow, Doree Marrical, Saundra Rietveld, Mary and Marven Norman, Mary Sewall and all the others for their many ways of sharing.
- Lee and Gary, Esther, Robin, Erin, Pat, Denali and Kelsey: for being family and allowing me elbow room to be my own peculiar self.
- Vera and Jack Green (Mother and Dad) and Grandma Ida M. (Wiker) Smith: for giving me life and the gumption to question it.
- Hweig, Amorto, Jamie and the Hidden One for their unseen but strongly felt over-the-shoulder editing of my work.

Thank You!

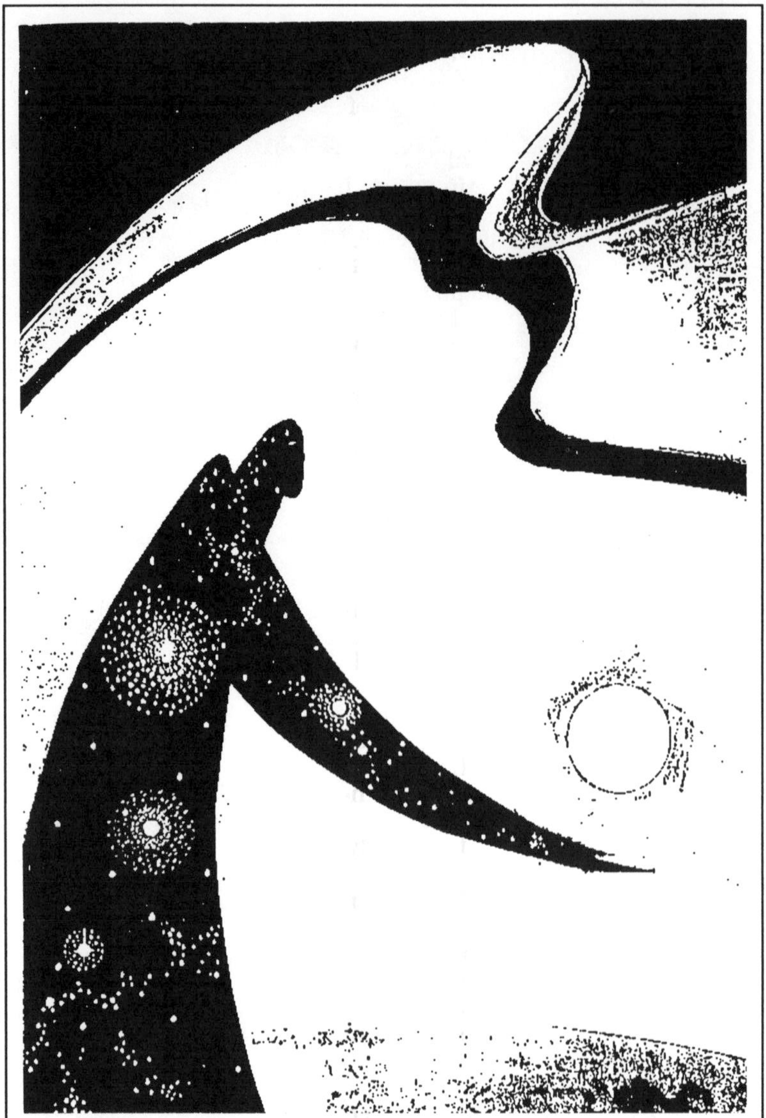

God Dreams

Do not come to Me with rote and ritual
Reciting books of someone else's prayers.
Has your soul no words of its own?

Why do you tag after me
Whining and whimpering like some
        tiresome brat?
        "I'm tired, I'm cold. I'm thirsty. I hurt.
        "Give me wealth. Give me fame.
        "Give me power?"
You are not pleading with Me
You are pleading against your fears.

Do you believe because I am God
        I cannot dream?
Or respect the dreams of others?

Do you see that pine tree
        there beside the river?
Before its first atom was born
        I dreamed it.
In all its perfection I dreamed
And the rocky hills, the curlew, the dawdling fish
        I dreamed them all.

You say you know Me?
Hmph! I do not know Myself.
Every second I change.
Every millisecond I become more.

Excuse Me, I go to find Myself.
I do not seem to be here.
I must have left Myself some place.

Be quiet then. Sit here on the rock
        Beside the waters
Meditate an hour or two.
Somewhere in your meditation
        I'll reveal Myself.

When your cries are stilled,
        Your heart at peace,
In Joy I'll come.
In Joy I dream.

        (Signed) God

Affirmation

"I have paid all my debts. I am free of obligation.
I do not need to hurt anymore.
I give myself permission to enjoy good health.
I give myself permission to be happy.
I give myself permission to love and to be loved.
I give myself permission to accumulate wealth.
I give myself permission not to worry."

Given to Ida
by
The Hidden One
February 22, 1993

Ida was also given instructions to repeat this affirmation several times a day until it was thoroughly ingrained. We could all benefit from following this advice and sharing it with the rest of humanity.

Books offered by Wild Flower Press

☐ **The Alien Book of Truth** — $7.95
  Who Am I? What Am I Doing? Why Am I Here?
  Author: Ida Kannenberg

☑ **UFOs and the Psychic Factor** — $12.95
  How to Understand Encounters with UFOs and ETs
  Author: Ida Kannenberg

☐ **Healing Shattered Reality** — $14.95
  Understanding Contactee Trauma
  Authors: A. Bryant/L. Seebach

☐ **Secret Vows** — $15.95
  Our Lives with Extraterrestrials
  Authors: Denise Rieb Twiggs & Bert Twiggs

☑ **Visitors From Time** — $16.95
  The Secret of the UFOs
  Author: Marc Davenport

☐ **The Aliens** — $5.95
  Cartoons by Olian
  Author: Helen Olian

☐ **The Talmud of Jmmanuel (TJ)** — $15.95
  The Clear Translation in English and German
  German Translators Meier & Rashid;
  English Translators: Ziegler & Greene

☐ **Celestial Teachings (CT)** — $12.95
  The Emergence of the True Testament of Jmmanuel (Jesus)
  Author: James W. Deardorff

☐ **Both CT & TJ as a matched pair** — $24.95

☐ **The TJ Database:** — $10.95
  ☐ Mac Filemaker Pro 3.5" disk, 800K
  ☐ DOS format text file 3.5" disk
  ☐ DOS format text file 5.25" disk

For more information about each book, write for a free catalogue. To order, check the books you would like and send a check, money order or put your credit card information in the space below. Thank you!

Mail to:

Wild Flower Press
P.O. Box 230893 Dept. ABT
Tigard, Oregon 97281

Ship the books to:
Name_____
Address_____
City_____
State_____ Zip_____

Please allow four weeks for delivery.
Prices are subject to change without notice.

POSTAGE & HANDLING
$2.50 for one item, $.50 for each additional item.
TOTAL FOR ITEMS $_____
POSTAGE & HANDLING $_____
TOTAL $_____

Send check or money order, payable in U.S. funds, or your
☐ M/C or ☐ VISA number: _____

expiration date: _____

_____
Signature

Documenting the Unexpected!